ON THE TRAIL OF
BIGFOOT

ON THE TRAIL OF
BIGFOOT

Tracking the Enigmatic Giants of the Forest

MIKE DUPLER

This edition first published in 2020 by New Page Books, an imprint of

Red Wheel/Weiser, LLC
With offices at:
65 Parker Street, Suite 7
Newburyport, MA 01950
www.redwheelweiser.com

ISBN: 978-1-63265-172-3

Library of Congress Cataloging-in-Publication Data available upon request.

Cover design by Kathryn Sky-Peck
Interior by Happenstance Type-O-Rama
Typeset in Adobe Caslon Pro and Caslon Antique

Printed in Canada
MAR

10 9 8 7 6 5 4 3 2 1

To my sister Jan
for letting me drag
her through the woods.

And to my grandkids:
Think for yourselves.

CONTENTS

INTRODUCTION

Thousands of people in North America and around the globe have reported encountering an unusually tall, hair-covered, upright creature that's something between man and ape. We have given these elusive and mysterious creatures, properly known as cryptids, myriad names, including Bigfoot, Sasquatch, Skookum, Skunk Ape, Grassman, and Wild Man. We have built narratives around them, logged countless blurry photographs and videos, cast what we believe to be their foot-prints, collected hair samples that lead to no conclusive identi-fication, recorded the sound of their distinctive whooping cries in the dark of night, and speculated about the creatures' habitat, diet, and social structures. But what do we really know about Bigfoot or any other cryptid running around in the woods?

Very little. We don't have bodies, or confirmed DNA sam-ples, or any of the kind of hard, empirical evidence that scien-tists need to identify these hidden creatures positively and study them scientifically. Without tangible proof—namely a living or dead specimen—professional scientists, for the most part, discount the reality of cryptids and dismiss the circumstantial evidence supporting their existence as misidentification at best, and as the work of hoaxers at worst. A handful of university scientists are willing to entertain the idea of the existence of large primates in the forests of North America, but those who attempt legitimate identification or study often face scorn and ridicule from their peers.

For hundreds of years, Native Americans have passed down stories of the great hairy men. For generations, people have told and retold tales describing creatures they consider to be very real and not just the stuff of myth and legend. White settlers reported encounters with "wild men" that fit the same description. We have pictographs and petroglyphs showing deer and fish—animals commonly seen in the environment in which the people who drew the petroglyphs lived. Alongside these, we sometimes see depictions of strange, large, hairy figures in the same naturalistic scenes, which would seem to indicate these creatures had a place in the artists' reality.

We hear strange sounds in the woods indicating something unknown. We find peculiar stick structures that seem to appear in the landscape like the obelisks from *2001: A Space Odyssey*. We have fleeting glimpses of large, dark shapes moving through the trees in ways that deer or bear don't move. We cast occasional tracks, but we still don't have definitive proof that these creatures exist. Those of us pursuing the mystery are like detectives trying to solve the perfect locked-door crime. We gather evidence piece by piece in our attempt to solve the mystery, only to have the clue that would tie the whole story together elude us.

Until professional scientists are willing to make a serious attempt at identifying and studying Bigfoot, it will remain up to novices and weekend warriors to collect the clues that will solve the mystery. Without us running around the woods looking for something positive to show the world, there would only be stories and legends. We have to gather information as best we can and build our case with every scrap of evidence we can find. Once we do find something—a track to cast, or a hair sample to analyze—we must use it to identify and describe the creatures we seek and to establish patterns or unique circumstances in which we can better understand what they really are. We need to gather the pieces of the puzzle in order to create a picture we can present to the scientific community to prove our case.

Persistent investigation will someday lead to the identification and protection of these gentle giants. We must work in an intelligent and cautious manner in order not to harm them or drive them farther away. As we go forth into the woods, forests, and swamps in search of these elusive creatures, we must proceed ethically to preserve nature and the integrity of these rare and unique animals. The purpose of this book is to add information that I have discovered to the body of evidence already found. Although my evidence is circumstantial, it all stems from my personal observation and not from pure speculation or imagination. I have used what I found to present the best argument I can for the existence of these creatures. Hopefully, those going into the field can build on my discoveries to understand them better and to recognize patterns that were previously not clear.

PROLOGUE

For as long as I can remember, I've been curious about the paranormal. I've been drawn to stories, movies, and TV shows about the strange, the weird, and the unusual. I finally reached a point in my life where I felt the call to search these things out for myself instead of leaving all the fun and adventure of investigation to others.

I started with ghost investigations after being inspired by the TV show *Ghost Hunters*. I've since been to some of the most haunted locations in the United States and have crept in the dark, infrared camera in hand, alongside the likes of Amy Bruni of *Ghost Hunters* and *Kindred Spirits* fame, and Kris Williams from *Ghost Hunters* and Ghost Hunters International. We did an investigation at the Morrison Lodge in Elizabethtown, Kentucky, which served as a Confederate field hospital during the Civil War. During my ghost-hunting adventures, I have concentrated on ghost photography, using special night-vision and full-spectrum cameras. I believe I have some of the best authentic ghost pictures in the world.

Several years ago, the mystery of Bigfoot caught my attention. In June 2011, I flew from Ohio to Washington State to visit my daughter, who lived and worked in the Northwest as a newspaper reporter. We decided to spend several days together and rented a cabin near Portland, Oregon. Together, we took a tour of the exceptionally spooky Shanghai Tunnels beneath the city. The tunnels are a haunted location that once housed countless men and women who were kidnapped from the streets above and sold into slavery or prostitution.

We stayed in a mountainside cabin in an Oregon state park about thirty or forty minutes outside of Portland. There, we had easy access to the city but could look out over a beautiful green valley while we feasted on breakfasts of fresh-caught trout and fried eggs cooked in cast iron over an open fire. The location gave us the best of both worlds and I highly recommend experiencing Oregon this way.

On one day of our stay, we decided to go see the Pacific Ocean. We headed west on Highway 26, which winds through valleys and the Coastal Range before opening up to the mighty Pacific and the sea stacks lining the coast. My daughter drove, so I had the chance to soak in the scenery. As I watched the landscape slip by, I spotted something that I recognized from my years of consuming all types of media about the paranormal, something that I knew was associated with Bigfoot in particular. Across a field next to the highway, there were several trees that had been pulled out of the ground and thrust back in upside down. I asked my daughter to pull over so I could take a picture and told her what we were witnessing. She was skeptical, but I knew what I saw. It was the first real, physical evidence of Bigfoot I had encountered in my life. This wasn't just a story to me anymore.

Figure 1. Trees stuck in the ground upside down, as seen in a field in Northern Oregon near the Pacific Coast. Legends say this is one of the ways Sasquatch marks its territory. I was actually fishing not far from this field, in Bigfoot's backyard.

That's when my personal search began. When I got home to Ohio, I started looking for any information about or evidence of Bigfoot that I could find. I discovered that Ohio is actually quite a hotbed of Bigfoot activity, with many sightings reported and much evidence found.

Thanks to my skills as a hunter and a woodsman, I've been able to find tracks and amass other incredible evidence of the existence of this creature, including some photographs. We'll talk about these as we explore the Sasquatch enigma together. Take a walk in the Bigfoot woods with an old ghost hunter and expect the unexpected.

1

From Ancient Astronauts to Dragons

A s intelligent humans, we have an insatiable need to understand our own existence. We have to know where we came
from. From the beginning, we have tried to reconcile the fact of
our existence with a burning desire to know our origins. How
were we created? Every culture has a story, myth, or legend to
explain the origins of our species. Almost every story concerns
deities coming from the sky and creating us in some manner,
breathing into us a divine spark. Perhaps our gods are seen as
coming from the sky because the heavens represent such a large
unknown. It makes sense that gods would populate such a vast,
mysterious place. Some of these stories of gods and goddesses
were used to control the masses, with priests warning the faith-
ful about jealous, angry, vengeful, or just fickle gods who had to
be appeased.

For entertainment, I enjoy watching television shows that explore the idea of aliens among us and ancient astronauts coming to earth. Those who theorize about ancient astronauts read myths and legends as true accounts of unearthly visitors arriving on our planet in our prehistoric and historical past. I tend to believe that these stories developed as a means to explain how we got here and why we exist. After all, ancient cultures provided the foundation upon which much of modern civilization was built, and our ancestors were no less capable of imagination or innovation than we are today. Consider how much of our concept of mathematics and science dates back to the ancient Greeks.

I believe that humans built the ancient monuments that dot our global landscape and don't agree with the notion that any of them were built by alien visitors. We have a hard time comprehending that our ancestors could have built amazing structures like the Egyptian or Mayan pyramids, because we fail to see how they could have done it without the benefits of our modern technology. We think we're superior. But it has been shown that Stonehenge could have been built by a few hundred men in a reasonable amount of time using levers and fulcrums, basic engineering principles that we still use today. If aliens came from untold light years away to show us how to build monuments, I'm sure they could have found better building materials than multi-ton blocks of granite. I think these kinds of suppositions demonstrate that, if we don't understand something, we just make up a story to explain it. We have replaced gods with alien astronauts coming down to bestow their gifts of technology, rather than giving credit to our own ingenuity as a species.

In a similar vein, I think we need to give credit to Native American cultures that, when telling stories about encountering hairy men in the forest, were actually describing something that was real to them. They saw something that walked like them, but wasn't them. They saw a creature covered in fur that looked like an exceptionally tall man. Because it is human nature to explain things that are unfamiliar, Native American cultures spun legends to explain what this creature might be and where it might have come from. But I do believe there was a kernel of truth at the heart of these stories.

GIANT BONES AND DOUBLE TEETH

Back in the 1800s, when settlers were clearing land to plant crops, they sometimes found large skeletons buried in the ground. It may be that what they found were simply larger-than-normal human bones. Since the average height back then was only five feet seven inches, any skeleton over six feet tall would have looked enormous to them. They did not know what to make of them. Having never heard of Bigfoot or Sasquatch, they thought they were the giants of the Bible. They called them Nephilim, after the sons of God mentioned in Genesis. They never thought to ask why giants from the Bible were buried in Ohio.

It is also true that, after the tendons waste away on a skeleton, the bones separate and can give the illusion of being longer than they actually are. This may account for some of the large bones found, but not all. There are reports of skeletons being found that were over eight feet tall, with larger-than-normal femurs and other bones. Some of these bones were misidentified as being from a giant, when it is more likely that they were from a mastodon, or possibly some other archaic animal, and simply gave the impression of being from a large person. There is nothing in the fossil record that indicates that a race of giant human beings ever existed. *Homo Heidelbergensis,* thought to be the largest human ancestor, was about six feet five inches tall, or perhaps a little taller. There have been scattered reports of relic Neanderthals possibly still existing in Russia, but it's highly unlikely there are *Homo Heidelbergensis* still running around in North America.

Once you account for large people, separated bones, misidentification, or even joint graves where bodies were buried together to give the illusion of a single large person, that still leaves some that remain unexplained. As with UFOs, once you remove the inexplicable, what remains is the mystery.

In ancient cultures like Greece and Rome, fossilized dinosaur bones may have been the source for stories about the giants and heroes of mythology. Perhaps they saw huge fossils sticking out from cliffs and hillsides and made up stories about mythological creatures to explain them. Myths of dragons, hydras, and cyclopes may simply have derived from the unexplained remains of stegosauruses, brontosauruses, and tyrannosauruses. The giant bones found in Ohio and elsewhere in the United States were not fossilized, however. They were old, but not fossils. This indicates that they were from no more than a few hundred years ago. That means that whatever creature they came from could still be around, unlike the dinosaurs.

One strange observation made about some of these giant skeletons is that some had double teeth. Since there is no evolutionary advantage to having two rows of teeth, this could be a mutation, not an adaptation. Or it may, more likely, be just a misinterpretation. In the past, before researchers had a base of knowledge or information with which to clarify observations like this, they often referred to things differently. Today, if we say someone has double teeth, we mean, literally, twice as many teeth. In the past, the term "double teeth" often referred to bicuspids and molars that appeared to be two or more conjoined single teeth. The term could also mean larger-than-normal teeth. "The giant had double teeth" actually meant that the creature in question had huge teeth. The term "double teeth all around" was often used to describe very worn teeth that appeared to be divided into multiple teeth. This was a common malady in the past when flour contained grit that was destructive to teeth. Likewise, when someone had very good teeth, which was unusual for the time, they were said to have double rows of teeth, meaning very good upper and lower rows of teeth. So what we have in the descriptions of these may be misidentification and misunderstanding that could account for some claims of giant skeletons, but perhaps not all.

If we look at these stories as a way for these cultures to rationalize or offer a reasonable theory about the "wild men" they encountered, we can understand that there may be an actual basis for them, and that they may be based on a real living primate. As we discussed, many cultures have myths and stories about dragons that may derive from dinosaur fossils found in hillsides and rocky areas. But the climate of North American was not conducive to preserving a fossil record, so we can extrapolate that Native American stories about a large primate in the woods were not based on gargantuan fossils, but rather on encounters with a real, living animal.

Because Sasquatch was such an elusive creature, many Native American stories bestowed upon them mystical powers, once again trying to rationalize something they didn't understand. They saw deer and bear and most inhabitants of the forests from time to time, and much of the game was hunted for food. But the hairy men were seen only briefly and on rare occasions. They kept their distance from humankind. This shy, elusive creature may have seemed inscrutable and been susceptible to mythologizing to explain it. Although most animals have a fear of humans, as deer hunters know, they don't go to such extreme lengths to remain hidden. Moreover, we find evidence of their existence in the woods—skeletal remains or scat—even when we don't see the animals themselves. Sasquatch leaves behind no such evidence, or at least not that we've thus far been able to find and identify positively.

GIGANTOPITHECUS

Some who research the existence of a large North American primate theorize that these creatures are descended from or related to the extinct giant primate known as *Gigantopithecus*, which lived in Asia as recently as 100,000 years ago. Some theorize that *Gigantopithecus* continued to live for tens of thousands of years and crossed the land bridge from Asia to North

America during the last Ice Age. Another theory states that, since *Gigantopithecus* lived at about the same time as human ancestors like *Homo Erectus* and *Homo Heidelbergensis*, this giant ape was hunted by early man. Some believe they were hunted to extinction because of the territorial needs of early humans. There is, in fact, a precedent for this in the fate of the Neander-thals. It is possible that remnants of *Gigantopithecus* crossed the land bridge to escape from humans, but ended up coexisting with them anyway. This could explain why they are so elusive.

It is also possible that pockets of *Gigantopithecus* remain in Asia, spurring stories of the Yeti and Yeren (see chapter 2). Clearly, something happened in the past to make these creatures so uncomfortable around humans. I believe that they are very intelligent, and that gives them the ability to hide from us the way they do. It would require an intellect superior to most other animals to remain hidden. I also think they hide in plain sight.

2

Our Family Tree

Taking a closer look at the fossil record of the giant ape known as *Gigantopithecus* that lived in China and existed at the same time as early humans. It is likely that there were some interactions between the ape and *Homo Erectus*, but to what extent we will never know. I can imagine the look on the faces of early humans the first time they saw a 10-foot-tall, 1,000-pound ape staring back at them. There are fossilized remains of both creatures located in cave dwellings in southern China and Vietnam. It seems as if their territories did overlap.

Gigantopithecus was discovered in the 1930s by paleontologist Ralph von Koenigswald while he was searching Chinese apothecaries for dragon bones. The fossilized teeth of extinct and ancient animals were often used in this region as medicines and curatives. While in Hong Kong, he came across the lower molar of a giant ape that was twice the size of the largest known gorilla tooth. He gave the ape the name of *Gigantopithecus Blacki*. This was the largest ape ever discovered. It had an estimated weight of over 1,200 pounds. Over time, more fossils were discovered. In the 1950s, a large mandible, hundreds of individual teeth, and several jawbones were found.

With this evidence in hand, researchers began to think of *Gigantopithecus* as a hominid along the lines of humans, but not a direct relative. How this giant ape moved about has been debated due to its immense size. One theory is that, because of its great weight, it would have to have been a knuckle-walker like a gorilla, since walking upright would have put too much stress on its hips and legs. Another theory is that, in fact, this creature's weight would have put too much stress on its knuckles and arms, so it would have to walk upright to distribute the weight. I'm no expert, but knuckle-walkers have a diverse big toe that allows them to pick up things and climb trees. Since they weighed over 1,000 pounds, however, these animals would have to have lived on the ground, because there wouldn't have been any trees stout enough to hold them. As ground-dwellers, I tend to believe that they would have been bipedal and would have adapted to that environment.

Zoologist Bernard Heuvelmans made a potential connection between *Gigantopithecus* and stories of the Yeti in the Himalayan Mountains. His hypothesis is that, if giant apes did not dwell in trees, it is likely that they took to the mountains to escape possible predators. Did *Homo Erectus* drive the giant apes out of the forest and into the mountains? The possibility exists. There would definitely have been a competition between the two species for territory and resources.

With the ever-increasing influx of Western mountain climbers into the Himalayas, the discovery of strange bipedal tracks has increased, raising the possibility that an archaic primate survives in the lush valleys between the remote peaks of this range and crosses over the snow fields to reach other valleys. A very interesting DNA study done by Dr. Bryan Sykes of the United Kingdom analyzed hair samples from two different areas about 600 miles apart and found that the samples, which were supposed to be hairs from a Yeti, contained DNA from an extinct polar bear. A jawbone from one of these bears had been found near Svalbard, Norway, where its DNA was extracted. All of the samples matched. This may very well have solved the mystery, or it may have deepened it.

The Sherpas and witnesses from the high country of the Himalayas know what bears look like, and the Yeti of myth and folklore doesn't quite match that description. What we may have, then, is more than one relic creature roaming the mountains. Polar bears wouldn't usually have ventured into the lower reaches where the Yeti have been reported. They would have resided above the snow line, feeding on lemurs and other prey. This bear was thought to have gone extinct about 40,000 years ago, but there could still be a remnant population in the high country, possibly coexisting with the Yeti.

Some noted scientists have considered the possibility of surviving populations of *Gigantopithecus*, or of descendants of the massive ancient primate, living in the dense jungles of southeast Asia. These creatures may very well have survived unnoticed by man. The absence of fossils does not necessarily equate to extinction. Another thing to consider is that *Gigantopithecus* is the only ape species that became extinct during the Pleistocene era. We assume this because there aren't any recent fossils or sightings of the animal. But indeed, they simply could have moved to another location, like the valleys of the Himalayas or the dense jungles to the south. Some probably crossed the land bridge into North America.

Some scientists have offered a theory that *Gigantopithecus* became extinct because it ate a specific variety of bamboo that became scarce, leading to the demise of the giants. However, others say that examination of tooth wear shows that they were generalized omnivores and that their diet was not that specialized. It is also possible that humans encroached on their habitat, forcing them to other areas to escape human contact. The fossil remains of *Gigantopithecus* relatives have also been discovered. *Gigantopithecus Giganteus* fossils have been found in northern India and China. This is a separate species that was only about half the size of its larger relative. *Gigantopithecus Bilaspurensis* lived in India about six to nine million years ago and was a large relative of *Gigantopithecus Blacki*. The closest relatives to *Gigantopithecus* living today are the orangutans. Any large cryptid apes living today could, however, be relatives of *Gigantopithecus,* or possibly offshoots of various relatives that existed in the same regions.

THE YETI

The Yeti is reported to be an ape-like animal, not a type of polar bear. The name "abominable snowman" was first used in 1921 to describe the beast. In 1832, mountaineer B. H. Hodgson reported to the *Journal of the Asiatic Society of Bengal* that some of his guides encountered a tall creature covered with long, dark hair walking on two legs, that ran away in fear. Hodgson believed it was an orangutan.

In 1899, strange footprints were found by Lawrence Waddell. His guides told him they were made by a large ape-like creature. Then, in 1925, N. A. Tombazi reported seeing a creature at about 15,000 feet in the Himalayas. He wrote that he observed the beast from a distance of 200 to 300 yards for about a minute. He stated that it looked just like a man walking upright and was dark against the snow. He later found tracks that were definitely from a biped.

In 1951, climber Eric Shipton took pictures of a series of footprints while attempting to climb Mount Everest. The pictures were taken at about 20,000 feet and have been the subject of debate for decades. At such a high altitude, they could very well be the tracks of the extinct polar bear, whose existence DNA testing confirmed.

In 1970, Don Whillans, a British mountain-climber, said he saw the creature while climbing Mount Annapurna. He was looking for a campsite when he heard some odd cries that his guides said were from a Yeti. Later that evening, he observed a dark shadowy figure outside his camp. Early the next day, he found human-like footprints and, later in the day, observed an ape-like bipedal animal foraging for food through his binoculars.

In 2007, Josh Gates and the *Destination Truth* TV series crew went to Nepal in search of the Yeti. They found a series of footprints that measured thirteen inches in length and had five toes. Plaster casts were made of the prints, but examination proved inconclusive.

The current theory proposed is that the Yeti is a bear or mis-identified bear, but eyewitness accounts tend to describe something more along the lines of a large unknown primate. The mystery continues.

THE YOWIE

In Australia, there is another possible relative of *Gigantopithecus* living in the brush of the outback known as the Yowie. The mystery surrounding this creature, however, is how it could possibly have gotten there. Australia broke off from what is now Antarctica about 95 million years ago, during the time of the dinosaurs. There are no primates native to Australia. The beast could not have evolved there, because there were no species from which to evolve. The aborigines say that the Yowie were the original inhabitants of the region, so they didn't bring them when they migrated there. And it's too far for them to have swum. A deep ocean trench called the Wallace Line that separates ecozones would have prevented aquatic migration. These creatures would thus have had to make boats and either sailed or paddled there.

We have reports of sightings of Sasquatch on Vancouver Island and other islands off the coast of Canada and Alaska, but those islands are near enough to the mainland that they could have swum there. Sasquatch have also been reported swimming in channels. But none of these observations can explain how the Yowie could have gotten to Australia. Some think they may have floated on fallen logs, but the distance is quite great for this. Moreover, such a migration would have to have included a breeding population. Not very probable. Yet there are numerous sightings of these creatures, possibly in the thousands. In fact, there are stories of British colonists seeing ape-like creatures that go back hundreds of years.

Those who know of the Yowie consider it to be intelligent, elusive, low in number, and inhabiting areas where there are few humans. Sound familiar? There have been attempts to capture or photograph them, but they have proven to be very smart and to figure out our tactics easily. They are thought to make stick structures somewhat like the Sasquatch, but cruder and different from those seen in North America. They may also use sticks as a way to leave messages or communicate. We can never know if *Gigantopithecus* made or used such structures, but it would be very interesting if they did, since this seems to be a behavior unique to cryptid hominids.

The belief is that the Yowie is a relative or descendent of either *Gigantopithecus* or possibly *Homo Erectus*. Some think it could be a giant marsupial. There was, in fact, a giant of this nature that existed up to 18,000 years ago called *procoptodon*. This massive animal was similar to a kangaroo, but stood about seven feet tall and weighed close to 500 pounds. The problem is that, if someone saw a giant kangaroo, they would probably recognize it as such. We know what kangaroos look like. And with hundreds of sightings, I think a pattern would have emerged. The Yowie is described as ape-like, not kangaroo-like, as the procoptodon was known to be.

A majority of sightings reported to be that of the Yowie depict a large bipedal primate covered in long dark-brownish hair. A proposed scientific name for the species is *Gigantopithecus*

Australis. This beast lives in dense forests and is thought to subsist on leaves, plants, berries, birds, and small mammals. Reports indicate that this is a curious, yet elusive, creature. It is said to use thumping sticks and rocks along with chest-beating to intimidate. Some claim that they use a form of chattering and gibberish to communicate. Here again, we have similarities to the Sasquatch. They construct short-term nesting sites by flattening areas of tall grass. The physical descriptions of them depict creatures with large red glowing eyes and a simian brow ridge. They do not appear to use fire or tools beyond sticks and stones and don't make permanent or semi-permanent nests or structures. This, again, could be a function of them being woodland creatures, living within their environment and not feeling the need to use anything beyond what nature provides. They are reported to have large noses similar to the Sasquatch. If you have seen the Patterson-Gimlin film (see chapter 10), you may have noticed that the nose on the female creature seems more human-like than the flat nose of a gorilla. They also have large canine-type teeth, which may explain certain tree bites that coincide with sightings.

It is curious to note that, while large canines are seen in the primate fossil record, they generally belong to non-bipedal species. This could be because these species split from quadrupeds in the distant past, but kept some of their basic traits. Many Sasquatch sightings do not include observing large canines, but this could be because the teeth were simply not visible. It could also be that large canines are a regional variation resulting from diet and genetics.

The footprints of Sasquatch in North America do not show a divergent big toe as prints cast in Australia do. These creatures could share a common ancestor like *Gigantopithecus*, but may have developed in different ways due to the vast regional distances. The Yowie's elusive behavior, however, is common to that of other cryptid large apes. Something clearly happened in the distant past to cause this reaction. Perhaps they were hunted or encroached upon and driven from their natural surroundings. Somehow, there seems to be a shared memory of human brutality that causes this behavior.

Almost every human culture has a story about a great flood occurring in the distant past. We find such tales in Sumerian legends, in the Bible, and in other cultures around the world. This may reflect a distant collective memory, which could be what the Sasquatch, Yowie, and other cryptid primates are responding to. If these creatures have a language, as some think, they could actually pass stories down from generation to generation. Various types of cryptid hominids are commonly reported to be somewhat nocturnal. They remain awake while humans sleep, are careful not to leave many tracks, hide when humans are present, avoid conflict with people, and chase away humans when they get too close to their young or their territory by throwing rocks or sticks. The Yowie could be in Australia because they were driven there by early man.

THE YEREN

In central China, a creature called the Yeren, which translates to "wild man," lives primarily in heavily forested areas. This is also the area in which *Gigantopithecus Blacki* lived. The animal is described as being between six and seven feet tall with thick brown or red hair. This could be a descendant or a variation of *Gigantopithecus*, but it seems to be a bit smaller. Footprints found measure about sixteen inches. It is not known or reported if they use or make stick structures, but it could simply be that we don't recognize these structures as being made by this creature. There have been numerous sightings over the years. In 1940, biologist Wang Tselin claimed to have seen the corpse of a female Yeren that was over six feet tall. He said the features were a cross between an ape and a human. It is not known what became of the body.

In 1961, workers building a road in the forest region of Xishuang Bauna reportedly killed a female creature. Here again, the body disappeared before scientific investigation could occur. Officials concluded that this was an ordinary gibbon, but years later, a journalist who investigated the report concluded that this was an unknown animal with a human shape.

In 1976, a car carrying local government officials encountered a Yeren on a rural highway. When approached, the creature disappeared up an embankment. An investigation followed, but nothing conclusive was determined. This creature was described as being over six feet tall and covered with thick brown hair. Its eyes were said to be human-like, but its face was that of an ape.

Biologists from East China University examined hair reported to be from a Yeren under an electron microscope, comparing it to hair from humans and different primates. They concluded that the Yeren samples were neither human nor from any known primate, but rather belonged to an unrecognized species that had human characteristics. It is quite possible that these creatures are taking over where their ancestors left off.

CRYPTIDS EVERYWHERE

In the Caucus mountains of central Asia, there are reports of a creature called the Almas, which is Mongolian for "wild man." This beast is considered to be more of a wild human than some kind of ape. The Almas is described as a humanoid biped that is five to six feet tall and covered in brown or red hair. Facial features include a flat nose and a pronounced protruding brow. These could be remnants of the Neanderthal, as opposed to descendants of *Gigantopithecus*. The fact that they are cryptid bipeds, however, puts them in the same category as Bigfoot or the Yowie. Sightings of the Almas have occurred for hundreds of years. In 1430, Hans Schiltberger recorded in his journals that he observed the beasts while on a trip to Mongolia.

In 1850, a wild woman was captured in the Caucus mountains and the claim was made that she was an Almas. Upon DNA testing of her descendants, however, she was determined to be of sub-Saharan African descent. Even though she was not an Almas, the legends of these creatures continue.

There are reports that Russian soldiers encountered a wild man in a cave in the 1930s. Thinking it might be a rebel soldier hiding out, the soldiers fired into the cave and killed the beast. Reports of sightings continue, and speculation is that they are either Neanderthal or *Homo Erectus* descendants.

In Vietnam, there is a Bigfoot-type creature called the Batutut. These creatures are referred to as the forest people. They have been encountered in the Vu Quang nature preserve and other jungle areas of Vietnam, Borneo, and Laos. Interestingly, work by Dr. John Mackinnan in this area has produced a number of newly discovered species of mammal. Mackinnan also claims to have observed tracks in 1970 that were attributed to the Batutut. He believes that an unknown hominid could very well exist in this area. He proposes that this could be a possible relic population of *Meganthropus*, an extinct ape that lived about 1.4 million years ago. This ape was large, but only about two thirds the size of *Gigantopithecus*. It is reported to be between six and seven feet tall and covered in hair except for its knees, hands, face, and the soles of its feet. It is usually seen foraging for food and is considered an omnivore because it has a taste for flying foxes.

During the Vietnam War, American soldiers encountered the animal and named it the rock ape. Professor Tran Hong Viet of Pedagogic University of Hanoi claimed that, in 1982, he found footprints similar to those found in 1970 by Dr. Mackinnon. Josh Gates of the SyFy show *Destination Truth* went to Vietnam with his team of researchers and found a series of human-like footprints that were cast and returned to the United States, where noted anthropologist Dr. Jeffrey Meldrum examined them. He described the prints as a "significant discovery. "

In Malaysia, another cryptid man-beast called the Orang Mawas (or Orang Dalam) has been reported. This creature is said to be a 10-foot-tall biped that is covered in black hair or fur. It has been seen raiding orchards and feeding on fish. Here again, we have an omnivore. Sightings of this creature go back to 1871 and continue into the 21st century. In 1995, large tracks were found in the Johr area. In 2005, a well-publicized account tells of three workers who were clearing an area for a pond near the Kincin River when they found a Mawas family of two adults and a juvenile. After the encounter, large human-like footprints measuring eighteen inches were found. In 2006, pictures of the prints ran in Malaysian newspapers and a government team was dispatched to the area to look for evidence. Thus Malaysia became the first country to mount an official investigation that attempted to identify an unknown hominid. The investigation was conducted without success, but the fact that it was done is very important. The theory is that this cryptid is a descendent or relative of *Gigantopithecus*.

Another mysterious primate called the Kaki Besar has also been reported in Malaysia. This is called the Bigfoot of Malaysia. It is said to be massive and covered with hair. In August 1966, newspapers reported that footprints had been found that measured eighteen inches in length and showed a stride of twelve feet. Local natives attributed them to a giant ape creature. This could also be some form of *Gigantopithecus*. It remains elusive and is seldom seen.

One would think that stories of Bigfoot-type creatures would abound in Africa, with the gorillas, orangutans, and primates that live there, but the closest example is a story about a mythical creature called the Chemosit. This beast has the hindquarters of a hyena, with the upper body and head of an ape. This hybrid animal is incredibly strong and eats brains. They are active at night and live in treetops. They can regenerate and jump for a mile. They sneak into villages and carry off victims, who are never seen again. This creature, of course, is pure mythology—a feature of witchcraft, along with its spells and potions. Native African religions portray evil, witchcraft, and monsters as working in opposition to the good—the old good-versus-evil narrative that has been the basis of mythology and religion for eons.

In South America, specifically in the Amazon rain forest, tales tell of a creature called the Mapinquari, a seven-foot-tall ape-like creature with red fur or hair, long arms, a sloping back, and powerful claws. The name translates to "roaring animal." Legend characterizes it as slow but ferocious and marked by a putrid smell. It emits a terrifying shriek, and arrows or bullets do not penetrate its thick hide. It avoids water, which limits its movements, especially during the rainy season. It is thought to be carnivorous. In 1937, it is said to have gone on a rampage and killed more than 100 cows. It avoids human contact, and there are no reports of humans being attacked. No physical evidence of the creature has been found, like tracks or hair, but in the environment in which it is said to exist, there might not be. Many believe the Mapinquari to be a character out of folklore, but others think it can be attributed to stories passed down about giant animals that once existed in South America. There are some who think this may be a Bigfoot-type creature. If it really exists, however, it is more than likely a surviving giant sloth, possibly mylodon, which lived in the Amazon about 10,000 years ago.

Another ape-like cryptid reported to live in the Amazon is the Maricoxi. Explorers came across these creatures in 1914. They supposedly lived in villages and used bows and arrows.

They were aggressive toward humans and attacked when they saw people, but were easily scared away by the sound of gunfire. They are usually described as being up to six feet tall, with some much taller. There are reported to be five different types of Maricoxi ranging from dwarfs, to evil ones, to wildlife protectors, to giants. It is likely that these entities are undiscovered or unclassified tribes living a primitive existence, rather than a distant relative of *Gigantopithecus* or some other hominid.

The Japanese Bigfoot is called the Hibagon. This creature inhabits the forest around Mount Hiba, from which it gets its name. It is described as being reddish-brown or black, with bristles on its face, a snub nose, glaring eyes, and an awful smell. Its face is protruding and long, unlike a human's. The Hibagon is said to be about five feet tall and weighs around 180 pounds. It is considered very ape-like, resembling a gorilla or giant monkey. It walks on two legs, but can easily walk on all fours. The first reports of the Hibagon were made in 1970, when the creature was seen by school children picking mushrooms. Later that same year, it was seen by a truck driver as it walked on two legs through a field. Strange tracks have been found on and around Mount Hiba over the years. Explanations include a mutated macaque or possibly an escaped orangutan. Another explanation is that it may actually be a feral human living in the dense forest. Increased hunting and human encroachment may also have driven some unknown animal from its habitat.

Another beast running around in Siberia is the Chuchunya, which is described as being six to seven feet tall and covered with long dark hair. Speculation is that this could be another relic pocket of Neanderthal, but its reported size makes it more likely that it is *Homo Heidelbergensis*, one of the tallest pre-human species, with heights ranging up to seven feet. To date, no evidence of the creature has been found.

An unfortunate incident occurred in February 1959 in the Dylatov Pass of the Ural Mountains in Russia. Nine college students on a ski trip were found dead, five of them frozen to death near their tent. The four others had mysterious injuries. One had a crushed head and one had a missing tongue. The scene looked as if the students had gotten up in the middle of the night, fleeing in terror. They left behind skis, coats, and all of their food. They were running for their lives in minus-thirty-degree temperatures. The investigation determined that they were victims of "a compelling unknown force." There were no tracks found because, by the time rescuers arrived, there had been a heavy snowfall. One theory is that they were attacked by a band of Neanderthals, possibly defending their territory. This case remains unsolved.

Literature is also full of references that may point to Bigfoot-type creatures. Beowulf, an epic poem dated between the eighth and eleventh centuries AD, describes the exploits of the hero, Beowulf, who was sent to aid Hrothgar, the King of the Danes. Hrothgar's mead hall was being harassed by a monster named Grendel, whom Beowulf ends up defeating. Some Bigfoot researchers theorize that the beast Grendel is based on a Sasquatch-type animal.

In the Bible, giants are described threatening the land and young David slays one with his slingshot. These stories may be based on sightings in Biblical times of possible relic populations of *Homo Heidelbergensis* or even *Gigantopithecus*. Sumerian texts speak of a figure called Enkidu, a wild man raised by animals who does not know human ways. Here again, the story may be about an unknown cryptid.

Thus, we have fossils of *Gigantopithecus* in China and stories of giant bipedal apes in the same regions. There are reports from China, Vietnam, Borneo, India, Nepal, and Tibet. There are gorillas in Africa, but there have never been any giant-ape remains found there. They seem to originate in Central Asia. We have accounts in North America of cryptid bipeds that probably crossed over from Asia on a land bridge. We have unknown creatures in Russia and the steppes that are probably relic populations of Neanderthal. We have primate-like bipeds in Australia that may be relatives of *Gigantopithecus*. Beasts in South America and Africa are probably misidentified animals or just folklore. Whatever the case, Bigfoot seems to have friends and family around the world. Even American legend Daniel Boone was reported to have killed a 10-foot-tall beast that he called a Yahoo.

3

Sasquatch Lloyd Wright

I am fascinated with the stick structures that some believe are the architectual creations of Bigfoot. Although I have never heard of anyone witnessing a Sasquatch building these structures, they do occur in Bigfoot-active areas. The only animals in North American forests capable of creating or building these teepee-style structures are either humans or Bigfoots. They are not something that deer, bear, elk, or any other four-legged animal could build. And the curious thing about these structures is that the ones I have seen, as well as the pictures of them I have found on the Internet, are all similar in design.

In the documentary titled *Bigfoot: The Definitive Guide* (see chapter 11), Dr. Ian Redmond spends time exploring on Vancouver Island and discovers a stick structure that he attributes to a Sasquatch. He described this kind of construction as being typical ape behavior, noting that a male ape might create such a structure to show other males that he is strong and can break trees, or perhaps in an effort to show dominance.

The structure featured in the documentary is of the teepee type that has reportedly been found all over the country—in the Pacific Northwest, in Minnesota, in North Carolina, in Ohio and West Virginia, and in Pennsylvania and elsewhere. There are various theories about what these structures may mean, if indeed they mean anything. Dr. Redmond believes that they convey intimidation and aspects of domination. Another theory says that they act as warnings to other Sasquatches that the area is frequented by humans. Others say they are built to mark territories by a male or family group. They may also be used as markers to identify potential feeding or breeding areas. Another explanation is that they may express artistic ideas. Just as early man used cave drawings, pictographs, and petroglyphs as an artistic outlet, these creatures may be doing the same thing, but in a different way. Without being able to observe the builders' behavior, we can only speculate as to the reason why tree limbs are arranged in this way.

PRACTICAL MEANINGS

My sister Jan and I decided one day to go to Salt Fork State Park in eastern Ohio to look for evidence of Bigfoot. When we got there, we had no idea where to look or what to look for. We started out walking a foot trail that went around a lake. We wandered up a ravine between two hills that seemed to have small caves in them. Then we sat on a log and looked around a bit, keeping our gaze sharp for anything that might indicate that a Bigfoot had been in the area.

It was October and the leaves were beginning to fall. My sister looked down and said, "This looks like a track." Sure enough, it did. There were several tracks that each measured about seventeen inches long. I took some pictures. One track had a perfect outline in the leaf litter. We had found tracks in the first place we looked! We left vowing to return.

Figure 2. A couple of tracks cast in Ohio. One was seventeen inches long.

The next spring, we returned to the same ravine, but found no tracks. Again, we sat there looking around and noticed that, on top of the hill next to us, there were several bent trees forming arches. We thought that this didn't look quite natural, so we climbed the hill. When we got to the top, we found more bent trees and a classic stick structure. This was a really exciting find for us as novice Bigfoot researchers. We took more pictures and looked for more tracks, but we didn't see anything definite. But still, in this one place, we had seen tracks, bent trees, and a stick structure.

I returned to the site again the following autumn and found two broken trees leaning at about a forty-five-degree angle to each other. The bent trees and the stick structure were still there as well. I took more pictures, of course, and looked for tracks again, but the terrain was not the best for finding tracks. It's mostly dry clay and leaf litter, so tracks aren't well-preserved and appear only as faint impressions in the leaves if they exist at all.

When I got home, I started looking at my pictures of the stick structure. The pictures had been taken at different times in different seasons, but from about the same angle. I lined up the trees in the pictures to compare the structures and noticed that they had been slightly rearranged. One of the sticks or limbs had been removed and another had been added. I considered whether the stick structure might have been made by a human, but I thought that, if a person had made this, there would be no reason to change it. No one would ever notice the change deep in the woods. I believed the structure had been assembled the way it was for a reason.

Figure 3. This is the stick structure first found by me and my sister. It was surrounded by bent and broken trees that might contain messages for other Bigfoots. Notice the branch behind the structure. It is missing in the next picture, which was taken about six months later.

Figure 4. The same stick structure as in the first picture, but taken six months later. Notice that the branch behind the structure seen in the first picture is gone and another stick has been added. What could this communicate to other Sasquatches?

I believe that these structures are used for communication. Any subtle changes could, therefore, convey some type of meaning. It could be that the bent and broken trees associated with the stick structure were part of the message as well. A Bigfoot might actually go to the hill and read what the signs meant. I have found three more stick structures and am watching them over time to see if any changes are made to them. I have noticed that, in the areas where I found the structures, there are always trees bent into arches close enough to the structures that they seem to be associated. Whether there is a meaning to them is unclear, but it is certainly worth investigating.

While doing Bigfoot research outside of Chillicothe, Ohio, I found another structure. This site is about 100 miles from the Salt Fork site, suggesting to me that the chance of someone perpetrating a hoax was remote. The structure was not exactly the same as the ones at Salt Fork, but it was similar. It was close enough in design that I believe both were made by the same type of creature.

What I also think is extraordinary is that the structure Dr. Redmond found on Vancouver Island and the ones I found are all similar. The pictures of the stick structures on the Internet from around the country are all similar as well.

I was on an expedition hunting black bear in Nova Scotia, Canada, led by Rob Bland, probably the best guide I have ever encountered. Rob offers world-class guided bear hunting and I recommend him to anyone looking for a wilderness adventure. There have only been three reports of Bigfoot sightings in the region where I was hunting since the 1800s, so I really didn't have any reason to look for Bigfoot sign. I was sitting in my tree stand (a fifteen-foot ladder stand) and, to my amazement, I saw a stick structure not thirty yards from my location. I had my camera phone in my pocket, so I took some pictures.

As the sun was going down, a large black bear came through the woods right under my stand. I waited until I had a good shot and fired my gun. The beast rolled, and I shot again. It rolled again, and I fired again. When it rolled the second time, it knocked down the stick structure. We followed the blood trail for about 500 yards, but eventually lost it and never found the bear. I told my guide about the stick structure and let him know he might have an angry Bigfoot in these woods.

I want to go back to Nova Scotia to see if the structure has been rebuilt or moved. The structure I saw there was in the

Figure 5. I took this picture with my phone from a tree stand while on a bear hunt in Nova Scotia. Too bad the bear knocked it over before I could get a closer picture. This is the only Bigfoot stick structure ever documented in Nova Scotia.

same form as the one I had found in Ohio, which is the same as the one Dr. Redmond found on Vancouver Island. And they are all the same design as the ones pictured on the Internet.

It seems extremely unlikely to me that the stick structure I found in Nova Scotia could be a hoax. We were in the middle of nowhere, where the only human activity related to the area was some commercial blueberry fields. My guide had cut a trail through the woods to set the bait stand, so this was not a trail used by or known to anyone but him.

Because all of these structures are based on the same design, known as the teepee design, I conclude that this building is learned behavior. If it were instinctive, the structures would be haphazard, without a common design. If this is a learned activity, however, then some form of intelligence and communication has to be involved. If it is learned, then the Bigfoots in the Pacific Northwest and the ones in Ohio and Nova Scotia and elsewhere must have passed this knowledge down from generation to generation. If they use these structures to communicate, than this is a form of learned language. Moreover, if this is learned behavior, then this language or form of communication is universal among the species, which is something we as humans have not achieved.

If these creatures change their structures to change their meaning or message, then any member of the species must be able to understand it. This may seem a bit much to infer from a pile of sticks, but the evidence is there. These structures are similar enough to be of the same design and origin, and the fact that the ones I have observed have been slightly rearranged suggests intelligent rather than instinctive behavior. The rearrangements are not something I believe could have been accomplished by wind or weather.

TEEPEE STRUCTURES

Some cryptozoologists believe that teepee-type structures may be used to mark territories. The ones I have found are located fairly close to human activity—not necessarily human habitation, but rather locales like trails, camping sites, and parking areas. The structure I found in Nova Scotia was located on a trail that led to a bear-bait hunting site. As we have seen, gorillas are not territorial. They defend the group as opposed to established territory. So if Sasquatch uses these structures as a form of territorial marker, this is more human-like behavior than gorilla-inspired activity. Primates in general don't usually defend territory, as they move from one area to another following food resources. Sasquatches have been known to throw rocks at intruders, which may indicate the defense of territory, but it is possible that defending or marking territory is simply the result of human encroachment on areas frequented by Sasquatch.

While other animals, like deer who relocate to avoid encroachment or bear who use human advances on their territory as an opportunity to scavenge our garbage cans, Sasquatches may retreat and claim lands on their own, setting up structures as a warning for us to stay away or be pelted with rocks. The placement of teepee structures in areas where humans would encounter them could be their way of warding off the human menace. The problem with this theory is that the vast majority of humans who encounter these structures have no idea what they are. If they come upon one in the woods, they just think it's a bunch of logs leaning against a tree. It actually takes a trained eye, someone who has encountered them before, to recognize them for what they are. In fact, there are actually people out there who hunt for Sasquatch, but don't have a clue how to recognize these stick structures. They look for tracks and Bigfoot sightings and don't mess with the rest. As I have stated before, I believe there is a wealth of information to be had from studying these structures.

It is possible that these teepee structures are not intended for us at all. The construction of these structures could be

Figure 6. Classic teepee structure found in various forms across North America. This one is located in Ohio.

intended to mark territories for other Bigfoots to identify. They may let family units know that they are in another group's area. Thus, the meaning of the structure could be a sign to avoid this area, or it could be an invitation to visit and intermingle with the host group. Since the groups are so scattered, this could present opportunities to mate, or just to learn about what is going on in other parts of the country. If Bigfoots use established trails and routes, then this may be a way to connect with other family units. If rearranging the structures could change a message, then rearranging the logs and branches could convey changes in locations or members of the unit. If the family group in the marked area had to relocate for some reason, the new location could be relayed through these rearrangements.

These structures may also be used to stake a claim on land. We have read about the Kensington Rune stone being an ancient land-claim marker. Perhaps Sasquatch uses these structures to accomplish the same thing. One could be placed at the border of claimed land, while several others might be located to mark the perimeter of the land being claimed. The number of logs or branches may indicate the area of land in question. Any Sasquatch passing through the area would need to show respect for the land and the family group residing there. These land-claim structures may also tell what resources are located in the area. A couple of stick structures I have found seemed to be fairly old, with the logs turning gray with age. Whatever the message they are conveying, it has been there for some time.

Could these structures possibly have these types of meanings? I really think that Sasquatch has the ability and is fully capable of doing such things. Their intelligence has always been implied by their actions. We will explore the fantastic creations made by these creatures, as well as the possibility of spoken and non-spoken languages, as we venture deeper into the world of Sasquatch.

Whether these structures are territory markers, or even something more complex or complicated like land claims, remains to be seen. Any of these explanations could make sense to an intelligent and reclusive creature attempting to establish territorial boundaries in relationship to a sparse and scattered population of fellow Bigfoots. If we look at the structures I have found in Salt Fork State Park, they could very well be boundary markers judging from the locations in which they were found,

Figure 7. Being watched by a Bigfoot guarding its territory.

and there is a possibility that there are more out there that I haven't found yet, which would reenforce such a meaning for the structures. The similarities among the structures leads us to think that they have a singular or specific meaning that only the Sasquatch can understand.

RITUAL MEANINGS

Another possible theory is that these structures may be ritualistic in nature. There is no known primate that uses ritualistic behavior. This is exclusively a human or pre-human trait. The oldest known occurrence of ritualistic behavior is the burial of an ax by *Homo Heidelbergensis*. The ax, which was nicknamed Excalibur, was placed in a grave, possibly for use in an afterlife. There have been several Neanderthal graves found that contain flowers and personal possessions or grave goods like bison and other animal bones and pigment ochre. The oldest actual burial that was done in a ritualistic manner is thought to be about 300,000 years old. This definitely makes it pre-human.

Since Sasquatch doesn't seem human, or even pre-human, the discovery of a ritualistic expression attributable to them would be totally unique. This might include a tribute, or recognition of nature, or worship of a deity. To think that these creatures could build or assemble something that honors anything spiritual is not out of the question. Could these structures therefore be altars to nature, or to a deity? They don't seem to include any adornment, nor do they contain any identifiable sacred elements, at least to our human eyes.

Yet I believe that the structure my sister and I found on top of the hill in Salt Fork State Park could very well be of a ritualistic or spiritual nature. The structure is in a very active area and is the centerpiece of the site. There are bent and broken trees that surround it, but the structure seems to be the focal point. The fact that the site changes, with items being moved, added, or removed, may be significant if this is a ritual area. Some of the anomalies we have found are varied and unusual. One log that was about twenty feet long and weighed several hundred pounds was placed against a tree. This log was there the first time we went, but the second time we went there, it was gone. We know that the log was placed against the tree and didn't just fall against it because there wasn't any root base. On our second visit, not only was the log not leaning against the tree, it had actually been removed from the site. It was gone altogether. We will never know if this log was removed as part of a ritual, but the way this site is laid out, it very well may have been.

The fact that the stick structure seemed to be the center or focal point of the site raises comparisons with human ritualistic areas. When an area is used for ritual, the focal point is often an altar. Perhaps the structure in Salt Fork served as an altar around which to assemble during ceremonies. The similarities of the structures could be a way to identify an altar area. Like many human ceremonial areas, these sites are usually circular, possibly allowing a group of people to face each other or concentrate on a central focal point. Stonehenge is a good example of this. In fact, there are many sites around the world that are similar and are used in the same manner. There are even round churches.

Stonehenge and other ritual sites are usually aligned with the Cardinal points, equinoxes, or solstices. It is unknown if any stick structure can be considered to align with any certain point or direction. I haven't yet researched this theory. One thing I have noticed is that, in the structures I have found, the main beam seems to go from high to low, from left to right, approaching from the "human side," usually entering from a path or trail leading from civilization. Whether this is intended or a coincidence is unknown. If it is intentional, then these sites are meant to be seen by us, in this way. But it is also possibile that they are aligned to something important to their builders.

One thing I have considered is that the stick structures may be memorial markers. It is thought that Sasquatches "bury" their dead, not in the way humans do, but rather by creating burial mounds. These structures may thus be the equivalent of headstones. I doubt if there is a Bigfoot buried under every stick structure, but it could be a memorial of a different kind. There have been reports of Bigfoots being seen in and around cemeteries. They may be curious about what our markers mean, or they may already know what they are. We erect statues to honor fallen heroes, important people, and community leaders. These structures may be intended as the same type of thing, in their own special way.

Another interesting hypothesis to consider is that these structures may be intended as a talisman to ward off evil. They may be thought to have magical or sacramental properties that can bring luck or provide protection from evil or harm. The structures may have been built with the intention of charging them with a form of magic to protect a family group from evildoers or even bad weather. They could be thought of as barriers that humans shouldn't cross lest they risk being cursed by woodland gods. The magical properties instilled into the structures could be part of a mating ritual, the spirits of the sticks engaged to ensure successful reproduction or to guarantee a male or possibly female offspring. This intention would make these structures not only ritualistic, but spiritual in nature. Evoking the spirits of nature for beneficial purposes may account for the gentle demeanor most Bigfoots portray, being elusive and non-aggressive. They may be the Hippies or flower children of the forest, professing peace and love. Groovy!

DOMINANCE AND DISPLAY

Dr. Ian Redmond conjectures that the structures he found on Vancouver Island are reminiscent of gorilla behavior, a demonstration of strength or a sign of dominance. I don't think this is quite correct. For one thing, if these creatures are breaking trees as a sign of dominance, why would they arrange them in a manner that is similar to other structures found all over North America? The placing of the logs and branches is purely intentional. Moreover, Sasquatch populations are scattered and sparse, often traveling in family units. Who are they trying to impress with feats of strength? Bigfoots are known to be territorial, but no conflicts among them have ever been reported. It is only when humans encroach on their space that they begin to throw rocks.

For many animals, display is a behavior that has been modified by evolution and is used to convey information. Animals display specific actions that other animals can use to interpret the mental or physical state of the first animal. To avoid the dangers of fighting, animals have evolved intricate rituals that are displayed to opponents to encourage them to back down or flee. The benefit-to-cost model of display assumes three things. First, the type of display will vary depending on the cost. Second, the risk of the display increases with its effectiveness. And third, the value of the resource being disputed determines the type of display used. Animals have evolved to utilize physical attributes as a display of ability. If altercations can be avoided with ritualistic display, then fighting can be avoided. Displays of strength or dominance can be used in disputes over mates, territory, or food, and these gestures can be used to avoid fighting. If an animal can intimidate without fighting, showing that it is superior to its opponent, then it can gain more by avoiding a fight than it would by fighting and risking injury.

In reference to Ian's statement that Bigfoot may be imitating gorilla behavior with the breaking of trees as a show of dominance, male Western gorillas also display a range of both vocal and gestural communication when a threat is present. These are used along with intimidating displays of strength. The alpha male will use chest-pounding, throwing, leg kicks, hooting, and sideways running when approached by another male. This show of physical abilities allows intimidation without actual physical contact. While this threat behavior could be considered to signify hostility or intent to cause harm, it is actually meant to challenge an opponent to back down or retreat.

The use of ritual display can have different meanings, while the use of threat behavior is meant strictly for hostile acts, even though it usually doesn't involve physical contact. Actual fighting doesn't happen very often because of the risks to both participants. On the rare occasion when fighting does occur, it usually involves individuals who are somewhat equal in size, or when the contested resource is necessary for reproduction or survival. Even when fighting does occur, some restraint may be used. The breaking of trees and the use of intimidating behavior is a defense against intruders of the same species or a defense against other predators in the area. The fact that Sasquatch populations are low and that they are the alpha or apex animal in the forest leads us to believe that this type of behavior is unnecessary.

The notion that Bigfoot would use the breaking of trees as a show of strength is more than likely incorrect. The piling up of logs in a teepee fashion is probably not a show of dominance. Superimposing gorilla-like behavior on Sasquatch just doesn't seem to work. The teepee structures attributed to Bigfoot don't seem to fit into any behavior patterns of any known animal. The legitimate scientists attempting to study this animal in the field, despite probable ridicule for doing so, tend to apply what they know of similar species, believing the species to be a variation of what they know. But facts keep surfacing that suggest that this animal is unlike anything ever studied. I commend the experts in the field, but they need to start looking at this as something totally different.

Of course, since they are found in the middle of the woods, there is a possibility that these stick structures are purely natural. I was deer hunting in Wayne National Forest in southeastern Ohio when I noticed what looked like a classic stick structure. After I sat for a while and determined that I wasn't going to be lucky that day, I walked over to the structure for a closer look. I have hunted that area for a number of years and, unlike Salt Fork, have never seen any Sasquatch sign there. I approached the anomaly carefully, looking for tracks or any other evidence that something might have left. I looked around and didn't notice any of the bent or broken trees that are often located with stick structures. Not all teepee assemblies have these elements associated with them, but most seem to. I wondered whether a family group might have moved into the area, which would explain why I hadn't seen any deer that day. Maybe I should change my tactics.

As I approached the assorted log pile, I checked to see if any of the fallen trees had a root base that would indicate a natural tree fall. They did. This was just a natural formation that looked like a classic teepee structure. To say that all of these struc-tures are natural, however, is certainly incorrect. I have located six, none of which, upon investigation, seemed natural. There weren't any root bases associated with them, which indicated that the logs and branches were placed intentionally. I can only speak for the structures I have found. But anyone finding these structures in the wild must look for this kind of evidence to see if they are natural or not.

PLAYFUL MEANINGS

The structures associated with Sasquatches may also indicate the playing of games. Imagine the sticks being the goal, or cen-tral point, of a game played by Bigfoot children or adolescents.

The home base for a "tag, you're it" type of play. Sasquatch could have watched native Americans as their tribal units played their own versions of games, which were often associated with their gods. They played ceremonially to try to ensure good harvests, bring rain, ward off evil spirits, or honor the gods by encouraging physical fitness. Although games were played for fun and enjoyment, there was usually a lesson to be learned to develop needed skills. Boys and girls usually played separately, playing variations of the same game but with different rules. Females didn't participate in games that involved hunting or warfare, but had their own games, playing house using small teepees and playing with dolls made from wood or corn husks to develop child-care skills.

Perhaps Bigfoot imitated this behavior in stick structures. Games were often played as fundamental learning experiences to teach younger members of the group the skills needed to survive and pass on these lessons. Maybe Sasquatch watched and realized that this was an effective way to teach their own young the basic skills needed to exist in the forest. Perhaps they used this information to develop their own games, using the stick structures to target whatever skill they wanted to teach, whether to defend a goal or to learn about parenting.

There are those who believe these stick structures are not made by Bigfoot at all, but are just forts and play areas made by imaginative children. Just kids playing around. When I was growing up in Ohio, we all played by a creek in a wooded area. We certainly did our own share of building forts and that type of thing. But we never built anything like a stick structure. We never saw anyone else build anything like it either. In the places

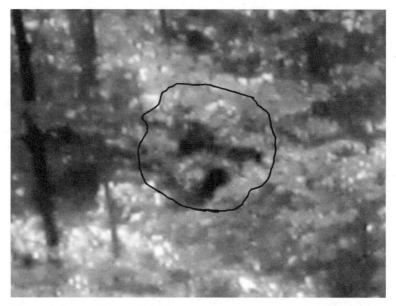

Figure 8. Curious Sasquatch eyeing every move.

where I have found these structures, it is unthinkable that children could have done this. The structure I found in Nova Scotia was definitely not made by children. So I don't think this explanation has any merit.

INTELLIGENT BEHAVIOR

Some believe these creatures are just lumbering brutish apes who make these structures without intent or design. Some think they are just unintelligent creatures wandering around in our woods. They liken Sasquatch to a mountain gorilla, existing purely on instinct with limited cognitive abilities. I don't think that type of animal could create these structures, nor bend and arrange broken trees, for no other reason than just to do it. No other primates build structures that are so similar to each other that they could be leaving messages or communicating through them. No other primate leaves behind anything that could be considered ritualistic, or even artistic. To say this is simply mindless stick-breaking is unreasonable. There is a basic intelligence at work creating these enigmas, for whatever purpose. They are planned and constructed for a reason. They have bent trees and broken trees and branches and other anomalies associated with them. They are changed from time to time, possibly to change a message or to update it. They express an idea and are not the result of an animal relying on basic instinct.

The possibilities expressed here are only guesses as to what these structures may be, or why they are built. Bigfoot is the only one who knows why they are there. We need to study these structures and try to decipher them to get an idea of how intelligent this creature really is. We may not have the ability to understand how these creatures think, since we cannot think in purely simplistic terms, but we need to understand that they *do* think, which means they could be our equals. When it comes to animal intelligence, we can only learn by observation. We are not Dr. Doolittle and we can't talk to the animals. They probably don't want to talk to us anyway. We need to redefine our concept of intelligence when it comes to other species.

Alligators have been observed with sticks on their snouts near flamingos that are building nests. The alligators wait until the birds get close enough to try to snatch the sticks for their nests. The alligators then ambush their prey, having lured them in. Similarly, monkeys use sticks to collect termites.

An interesting study from the University of Adelaide in Australia states that reasoning is just one form of intelligence. Some animals leave some form of scent markings in order to communicate, which is foreign to us as humans. Killer whales are known to have a complex language, and dolphins use whistling signals to identify individuals. They have a concept of self and recognize others. Elephants have excellent memories and grieve for their dead. Beavers build underground homes and dam flowing rivers. Bees do a dance to show others where nectar can be found.

Life exploded on this planet about 400 million years ago and, since then, millions of species have developed and evolved. Out of all of those species, we are the only ones that we know of who have created their own artificial nature. I once read that intelligence is the ability to adapt. I think we need to add to that definition the ability to survive. Take, for example, monkeys using sticks to get to termites or alligators using sticks to lure prey. This is problem-solving in order to survive. These animals are creating additional opportunities to eat and survive, rather than waiting for a natural opportunity to present itself. We could also look on this as planning for the future. They use certain techniques to obtain food so they can eat when they are hungry. They are planning their next meal. This demonstrates cognitive ability, although in a limited sense.

We cannot say we are smarter than other animals. Creatures are intelligent each in their own way. A grizzly bear can't build a rocket to the moon, but he can smell a salmon through six feet of ice. Try doing that.

APPLES AND ORANGES

At a Bigfoot conference at Salt Fork Lodge in eastern Ohio, I attended a lecture by Dr. Esteban Sarmiento on the topic of feces. He believes that Bigfoots are primarily vegetarians and would be very surprised if they hunted. He recommends looking for feeding areas and trying to find fecal remains that could tell us quite a bit about their feeding habits and could also possibly contain DNA. I have looked in places that should fit this description, if that is indeed their behavior, but I didn't find anything. It makes more sense to me that these creatures are omnivores who hunt prey. There are too many reports of them stalking or harvesting deer to discount the idea of Sasquatches as hunters. There are many reports of Sasquatches throwing rocks. These powerful animals could use that technique to take down a deer from a fair distance. An individual or a small group could survive rather well this way.

It may be that Dr. Sarmiento is comparing Sasquatch to the gorillas he has observed in the wild, where groups consume large amounts of vegetation every day. I respect his expertise with primates, but, in this instance, I think he may be comparing apples to oranges.

If Bigfoot is related to the great apes, then either their behavior has changed dramatically or they are distant cousins. Great apes are knuckle-walkers, which some scientists think is a mutation rather than an adaptation. Bigfoot is reported to be bipedal, only traveling on all fours on rare occasions. Gorillas are primarily vegetarian, whereas Bigfoots are said to be carnivores or omnivores and have been associated with deer kills. Bigfoots seem to be territorial and have been known to throw rocks at intruders, while gorillas do not. Bigfoots are thought to travel in family units consisting of a male, a female, and one or two young, while gorillas travel in troops. Bigfoots are thought to be nocturnal, while gorillas sleep at night. The differences in behavior and physical attributes lead us to think that they are far removed from gorillas on the evolutionary scale. Gorillas use guttural noises as commands, where Bigfoots are known to use a form of language some call samurai chatter (see chapter 4). They are not the monkey's uncle.

We can find mountain gorillas. But we can't seem to find Bigfoots. I live in Ohio and these creatures are right in my backyard. Yet, but for some fleeting glimpses and circumstantial evidence like tracks or stick structures, they might as well not exist at all. But I know they do. In the animal kingdom, the reaction to human presence or encroachment is to either flee or assume a defensive stance. I was once walking in a reported Bigfoot hotspot taking random pictures of the surrounding woods to gather photographic evidence. Upon reviewing my pictures, I was amazed to see that I had captured, in four separate shots, a total of four Sasquatch concealed in the brush! They were watching me, and I was totally unaware of them. They did not flee or become defensive, they just watched as I moved through the area. This is not typical instinctive behavior. They were either curious or protective, which indicates intelligence.

Figure 9. Stealthy Bigfoot peeking from the brush.

Even some of the rarest endangered animals are seen from time to time. How can Bigfoot be so elusive? The tracks I have found are not all miles back in the wilderness. I found some less than a mile from a road or human contact. They seem to hide in plain sight. This indicates intelligence. They are known for traveling in areas where it is hard to leave tracks. They seem to be able to see and locate camera traps. We think that, to be intelligent, animals must think the way we do. We are wrong.

Bigfoot knows us. They know our actions and how we react. They have been watching us for centuries. We think they are nocturnal, but there are very few nocturnal primates in nature, and those who are have developed special adaptations. On the other hand, Bigfoots could very well want us to *think* they are active only at night. They are patterning us.

I think Bigfoots may experience segmented sleep. There is a precedent for this in humans. During medieval times, people had two periods of sleep. They slept for a few hours, then got up to do chores or visit neighbors, then slept for a few more hours. All of this changed with the advent of the Industrial Revolution, when people migrated from rural areas to cities and started working at jobs instead of working the land. They had to shift to sleeping at night and working through the day.

I think Bigfoots may sleep in sessions lasting a few hours and then get up to feed or move about or even socialize. We think that, since they don't use tools or fire (to our knowledge), they are unintelligent. But they are woodland creatures. They don't feel the need to create an artificial nature in which to exist. They live within the confines of their natural environment. They use what is at hand to carve out a life. They use rocks to ward off intruders like us. They use sticks and branches to communicate, either by building structures or hitting tree trunks or logs. They make shelters from what's available.

I found what some would call a nest that was located about fifty yards from what is known as a bent tree nest. Here, pine trees were bent over to form a single shelter big enough for perhaps one creature. In all, the area contained shelter for about four individuals. I don't think these structures were intended as living quarters, but rather as temporary shelter from bad weather. They were probably placed in various locations that were easy to reach in case bad weather moved in. I really don't think we have actually found a Bigfoot living area yet. They know where to put them so we can't find them, or else they hide them in a way that makes them unrecognizable to us. The shelter area I found coincides with current theory held by some that Bigfoots travel in family groups. This makes sense as a survival strategy. A dominant male or female could provide for a small group with less effort than trying to provide for an entire tribal unit.

If, in fact, they range within established territories, these creatures could communicate either through tree knocking ("Hey . . . I'm over here!") or through stick structures. Trees bent or broken in one direction could convey a specific meaning, while those bent in another direction could convey a

Figure 10. Suspected Bigfoot nest found in eastern Ohio. This structure was big enough for me to stand up in. When I returned to this same area some time later, the nest was no longer there.

different meaning. Stick structures could do the same thing. The changing or rearranging of stick structures could signal a specific activity. For instance, changing the stick location in one structure could signal mating season or some other activity.

FOLLOWING THE FOOD TRAIL

As woodland creatures, Bigfoots live within the balance of nature, taking only what they need and leaving nature as they found it. Greed is a concept unknown to them. They observe us and our technology and shun us at all costs. It seems as if the prime motivation of their activity is to remain hidden from us. This raises another question that goes counter to everything we have just discussed. Why are they where they are? Why are they in Salt Fork State Park in Ohio? You would think by their actions that they would go so far back in the wilderness that we would never see them. Yet here they are in my backyard. For some reason, they make the effort to occupy this park and, at the same time, choose to remain hidden.

Several years ago, the Animal Planet show *MonsterQuest* told the story of a cabin in northern Canada situated by a lake. It was only used at certain times of the year and the rest of the time remained unoccupied. To dissuade bears from rummaging through the cabin when he wasn't around, the owner placed boards with nails sticking out of them on the ground in front of the door. Upon returning to the cabin, the owner found that one of the boards had been stepped on. There was hair and blood and bits of flesh on the nails and board. The owner contacted Bigfoot investigators and submitted the board for DNA testing. Ultimately, the DNA samples were too degraded to offer any evidence.

In the meantime, while waiting for the DNA results, the *MonsterQuest* investigators went to the cabin and set up camp. After several days of doing various research projects, they settled in for the evening, ate dinner, and relaxed. During the evening, they were startled by something throwing rocks at them. They were in the middle of nowhere and had had to fly to this location because that was the only way to access the cabin. There were no other people around to pelt them with rocks. They actually heard one land on the roof. They were quite unnerved by this. Soon, the rock-throwing subsided and they turned in for the evening. They left soon after, vowing to return.

The next year, the group returned to the cabin and, after several days, hadn't encountered anything unusual. They were told that there were sightings about 100 miles south of them and noticed that blueberries were ripe in that area, although the berries had not quite ripened in the area farther north where the cabin was located. They theorized that Sasquatch could be following the food trail as it advanced north. Indeed, it makes sense that they would migrate following the food supply.

The stick structure I found in Nova Scotia was pretty much in the middle of nowhere. I asked my guide how much territory the woods covered, and he told me they stretched for miles. Then I noticed the presence here and there in the woods of large commercial blueberry fields. I believe the berries had been harvested before we got there, because we didn't see any workers, but there were still a few blueberries on the bushes.

That is why there are so many large bears there, because of the blueberries. Coincidence? I don't think so.

So what about Salt Fork? There aren't any blueberries there, but there are blackberries and black raspberries that ripen at different times. And I have noticed that there is more sassafras there than any other place in Ohio that I have seen, and I have been hunting deer in Ohio for forty years. If you are not familiar with sassafras, it has a very aromatic root from which you can make tea. The original root beer or sarsaparilla drinks were made from the root. The entire plant is edible, but to smell and taste the root is heaven. I think the big hairy one has a sweet tooth and that could be why he lingers in Salt Fork. The roots can be harvested summer or winter.

So here we have a creature that may migrate following certain food sources, perhaps berries and sweet-tasting foods. And we also have stories of Bigfoot harvesting deer, which are plentiful in most American hardwood forests. They may have the ability, through rock-throwing and sheer strength, to bring down deer and other animals without much effort. This again adds to the mystery of how even sparse populations of any animal can migrate from one area to another, whether to follow food sources or for other reasons, without being seen. How can they do that?

In Ohio, a Bigfoot has been observed that had a whiteish color to it. Some think that some Sasquatch may remain behind in the home territory because they are older and can't travel. There may be some that are very young and can't travel well either. There is plenty to eat in this area, even in the winter, for those who stay behind. There are deer, sassafras, cattails, and other aquatic plants that they can harvest by breaking the ice. We believe that most able-bodied Bigfoot do travel. As we have seen, however, there seem to be some noted differences between them and gorillas. We haven't established any defined or concrete patterns for Bigfoot behavior, but we can infer a type of behavior from sporadic observations and by connecting the dots in a logical manner.

MORE APPLES AND ORANGES

In his book *The Mountain Gorilla: Ecology and Behavior*, noted biologist George B. Schaller describes patterns of movements observed in several groups of mountain gorillas over an extended period of time. Most of the movements were highly irregular and there were no predictable patterns. Although the movements were within the boundaries of their home territories, their arrival in one section or another was totally irregular. The departures and arrivals in certain areas varied with each group, with no definite pattern shown. Certain groups remained in areas for one or two days, some for nearly a month. Several groups displayed recurring trends, but they almost always used different paths to reach a destination. Even though different groups traveled from one area to another, they took a different direction almost every time. There did not seem to be a specific route, however, which shows a wandering nature as opposed to definite migration patterns.

The direction of travel for any given day was also quite unpredictable. Although a group sometimes followed a general route, they quite often veered off and took other paths. The distance traveled on a given day also varied widely. Some groups traveled about half a mile while others traveled from three to seven miles. One group observed moved only 300 feet. The distance traveled seemed to be determined by the individual leaders of each group.

According to Schaller, the distance traveled by a gorilla group can sometimes be correlated with the abundance of food, but not always. One group spent quite a bit of time foraging for bamboo, while another group moved to an area where food resources were negligible. What has been observed is that a group of mountain gorillas follow what the dominant male or leader of the group does or wants them to do. Since these animals are primarily vegetarian, food sources are seemingly abundant and traveling for the sake of finding food is unnecessary. Even though they are displaying what we might think of as instinctive behavior, they are actually using cognitive abilities to maintain a social order that ensures their survival. Without the leader or dominant male to follow, many would just wander away, which would affect mating and the continuation of the group.

When we think of a family group of Bigfoots migrating from one area to another, probably following various berries as they mature, it seems safe to assume that they do this by choice, a choice driven by desire rather than necessity. If they are omnivores, as many researchers think, then they probably could exist in family units in certain areas like Salt Fork without the need to migrate. With plentiful deer, aquatic plants, water, streams with fish and crayfish, and berries to subsist on, the need to move would be negligible.

If these creatures travel to different areas because of something they want, then they must have established travel routes. This is supported by the simple fact that they are so elusive. Specific routes would make it possible to remain hidden from humans. They would need to know how they could get from here to there without being noticed. They would have to know where people were in order to avoid them. But we humans are always changing, building new houses and apartments, moving about. Bigfoots would have to know this and communicate this to others in order to remain hidden. This is a different type of behavior from that of mountain gorillas following a dominant male wherever he goes. What we see here is discipline and planning. If these creatures exist (which I fully believe), then this has to be the case. You cannot wander the countryside haphazardly and remain hidden. Apples and oranges again.

Gorillas are also diurnal. They are most active during the day. Most Bigfoot researchers believe that Sasquatch is nocturnal, an idea with which I disagree. While it is true that a lot of sightings have occurred at night, I think this may be because of segmented sleep. These creatures do move at night, but their nocturnal activity may very well be social in nature. Without special nocturnal adaptations, like eyes that can see well in the dark, it would be very difficult to hunt at night or recognize specific foods to eat. If Sasquatches use rocks to take down prey, I'm sure they do it during the day, probably during the early morning or in the evening, when deer are moving to feeding or bedding areas.

Gorillas sleep through the night, sleeping for about twelve hours, and stay together in groups so they are less likely to be attacked by predators. There are reports that Sasquatches have a sentry that keeps watch while others sleep, and some of these observations were made during the day. Without specific data about their daily activity, it is difficult to say what actually happens.

To return to Schaller's work and the feeding habits of mountain gorillas, he observed that gorillas feed several times a day, with periods of rest between sessions. One of their major food sources is a type of vine named galium, which is abundant. In fact, most of the vegetation they feed on is available year-round, with only some being seasonal. The rubus fruit is eaten year-round, while the pygeum fruit ripens in April. In many areas, bamboo makes up the bulk of food eaten. Curiously, some of the foods eaten by gorillas are of meager nutritional value and the reason for eating them is unknown. It may be that some of them have medicinal properties, or they may just taste good. The important thing is that the foods eaten the most are readily

Figure 11. Bigfoot sentry perched in a tree.

available and within easy reach. The bark and leaves of various vines, along with leafy fauna and bamboo, make up the bulk of foraged food, while cultivated bananas, peas, and corn are eaten as well.

A lengthy study of mountain gorillas' eating habits showed that their diet consisted of 4 percent grass, 5 percent ferns, 29 percent herbs, 22 percent vines, 9 percent shrubs, 25 percent trees, and 6 percent cultivated plants. Of the large number of plant species eaten, only about a dozen provide most of the foraged food. Gorillas actually only eat a small percentage of the plant species available to them, and the most abundant plants are usually not eaten. The plants they do eat are usually readily available. It is interesting to note that gorillas don't eat many leaves of the plants they consume, but instead prefer to peel the stem to get to the center stalk, leaving the high-fiber bark and the nutrition of the leaves.

Gorillas occupy different environments and have adapted their feeding habits to these environments. Even though the same food-plant resources exist in different environments, one group of gorillas may not eat the same plants as other gorillas, even if they are available. This may be due to a dominant male's influence over the group when it comes to feeding habits. A dominant male may not particularly like a certain species of plant even if others do, but the others follow what the male does.

Gorillas eat primarily plant matter. It was thought that they might possibly eat termites, grubs, or bird eggs, but examination of fecal matter has not shown this to be true. Captive gorillas are fed and eat meat, but they do not typically eat meat in the wild. Gorillas in the wild eat readily available plants.

The hardwood forests of North America don't typically support the kinds of plants that gorillas eat. They don't usually eat leaves, but that is about all a primate would have to subsist on in our forests. Very little vegetation grows under the canopy of oak trees, mostly ferns and briars, which would provide limited food for an herbivore. There are aquatic plants available, but they could feast on deer with less effort. The notion of a Bigfoot family unit subsisting on vegetation alone, especially during the winter, just doesn't play out. Apples and oranges again.

4

How Does Bigfoot Communicate?

C ommunication. It is how we learn, how we teach, how we understand. Communication is essential to any creature's survival. Animals communicate in various ways. I believe that Sasquatch has developed several unique ways to do this. One is through stick structures and signs left in the woods so others can see and read messages. They use structures made of sticks placed in strategic ways, bent trees, and broken trees or branches to leave long-lasting messages for others to read. Changing the structures changes or enhances these messages, which may communicate changes in the location of family units, food resources, human movements or contacts, seasonal changes, or anything else they want to convey. Because they are few in number and somewhat nomadic or migratory, it makes sense that these creatures would use this type of communication, since established trails or paths are probably used to avoid human contact.

These structures and the altering of trees and branches go unnoticed by humans because we think they occur naturally. When I showed my bear guide in Nova Scotia the picture of the Bigfoot structure, he told me that it was just the way the logs fell, until I showed him pictures of others that were quite similar. It really got him thinking. If you don't know what to look for, you really don't pay much attention.

Lots of animals use scent to communicate and Sasquatch may also communicate through smell. There are reports of a foul odor being present when Bigfoots are around. This could elicit a sexual or provocative response in other Bigfoots, or it could also be a form of camouflage. The scent may come from something they apply or roll in, or it could be secreted. The use of scent could also be self-defense. An odor could be used to ward off humans, since there are probably no natural predators for the Sasquatch. A noticeable scent could alert humans to the presence of Bigfoot, telling them it was time to make a hasty exit.

These creatures may also communicate through telepathy or impressions. If they have the ability to do remote viewing (see chapter 5) or some type of astral projection (see chapter 6), they may be able to project a thought or information. Even though some researchers consider ESP (extra-sensory perception) to be pseudoscience, there is a sound basis for that research to be conducted and underlying questions still exist. Some types of elevated awareness may be inherent primate behavior that we dismiss because our thought patterns are geared more toward problem-solving than communicating to survive. Thus we may have suppressed this ability. As our numbers increased, our dependence on this type of ability may have decreased. If the

Sasquatch population is sparse and scattered, however, their need to communicate in this way may be greater, especially during mating season.

Bigfoots may also use infrasound, sound that is too low in frequency for humans to hear, to communicate. Although we cannot hear this sound, it affects our bodies, causing nausea, headaches, fatigue, blurred vision, disorientation, dizziness, and emotions like fear or dread. Lions and tigers use infrasound to freeze their prey before they attack. Infrasound may also be used as a warning mechanism to ward off humans. The government uses infrasound for crowd control. There are reports that, on some occasions during a Bigfoot sighting, witnesses have experienced some type of paralysis and temporarily lost the ability to move. This may be why some Bigfoots aren't shot. They have an innate form of self-defense.

Conversely, ultrasound, sound that is too high in frequency for humans to hear, may be a means by which Bigfoots communicate. In nature, bats use ultrasound as a form of radar that enables them to find food and avoid obstacles in the dark. Whales and dolphins also use it to communicate. Ultrasound may enable Bigfoots to move around more easily in the dark. If they do have this ability, it would make them unique among primates.

Another theory gaining ground is that Bigfoots may possess the ability to generate a static charge around them, like wearing a wool sweater and touching metal. What a shock! This could explain how a Bigfoot's eyes can glow without reflected light. How many times have we heard stories about someone seeing "eye shine"?

Tree-knocking or rock-clacking may be another form of Bigfoot communication. Striking a tree or log with branches can project sound for quite a distance, sound that could be used as a locating or "Here I am" signal.

Verbal language is, of course, the most common form of communication for humans. The origins of language are unknown. We can determine when we first physically obtained the ability to speak through fossil records, but it's impossible to determine when the first word was actually spoken. The use of language probably occurred when social orders were developed, making it necessary to communicate various ideas and commands when in hunting or survival situations. Social orders and artistic expression seemed to develop and grow simultaeously, introducing the need to express ideas. When language did develop, it probably occurred as regional dialects.

Whoops, whistles, grunts, growls, howls, screams, and a form of chatter have all been reported during Bigfoot sightings. Sasquatch are also known to mimic sounds of nature like bird calls or the sounds of other creatures. The often-reported grunts, whoops, and whistles may represent regional vocalizations, and the so-called samurai chatter, or phonetic language, thought to be used by Sasquatch may be colloquial. I wonder what the Bigfoot slang term for humans would be.

The interesting thing about Bigfoot stick structures as a form of communication is that they are basically all the same. As stated before, the similarities between the structure on Vancouver Island and the one found in Nova Scotia indicate that this has to be a learned activity. Although they may be described differently, the fact that most of these structures are so similar is strange. History shows that cultures on different continents and thousands of years apart built pyramids. Is this the same phenomenon? It is highly unlikely that the ancient Egyptians showed the Mayans how to build pyramids, yet they both built the same structures. And no, the aliens didn't do it! I think that ancient cultures built pyramids because it was the easiest way to make monumental structures. If you think about it, they could create very large structures without having to put a roof on them. Simple! Build the sides progressively inward as you go and you're done. Sounds easier than it is, but it's the way a lot of civilizations solved problems. They built the same structures because it was the best way to do it. They didn't have to learn it from someone else. They just figured it out on their own.

This doesn't seem to be the case with stick structures. They are simple, but they are too similar to have been made randomly. This seems to be a learned behavior. If they convey a message, then the message or meaning must be universal among Sasquatch. The structure on Vancouver Island means the same thing as the one in Nova Scotia. We are probably dealing with forms of communication and degrees of intelligence that are so foreign to us that they are unrecognizable as such. To teach something, you have to tell or show someone or something how to do what you want them to do.

SASQUATCH-SPEAK

There are instances in which Sasquatches are said to use a type of language. In 1971, a group of hunters built a hunting camp in the Sierra Nevada Mountains of California. Bill McDowell, Ron Moorehead, and Alan Berry constructed a crude camp consisting of a lean-to shack and the barest necessities. On occasion during their treks to the camp, they saw large human-like footprints that they thought were bear tracks, because bears will step in their own tracks, making them look much bigger. One evening after dinner, they were relaxing in the shack when they heard some banging and crashing noises outside. One of the men in the group grabbed his gun and was going to see what was making the noise, thinking a bear had gotten into their gear, when, all of a sudden, he heard deep guttural grunting sounds, snarls, and teeth-popping. He also heard what sounded like chest-beating, and what sounded like two creatures having a violent disagreement. This lasted about thirty minutes. After hearing the commotion, he decided against going outside. When the sounds finally subsided, they ventured outside to find pots and pans scattered about and some of their food gone. They also found a couple of eighteen-inch, five-toed human-like footprints. Whatever made the noise was a lot bigger than they were.

They closed themselves up in the shack and didn't get much sleep that night. The next day, they ventured out and took pictures of the tracks to confirm that this had actually happened. The next night, they set a trap to see if they could find out what was invading the camp. They cooked up some bacon and put cans on top of it to make a noise if anything tried to take it. They thought they could rush out and catch whatever was doing this. Later that evening, they heard voices and the sound of cans crashing, similar to what they had heard the night before. They rushed out and the only thing they saw was a large shadow moving through the woods.

The next morning, they packed up and headed down the mountain, keeping a watchful eye over their shoulders. Two of the hunters returned to the camp a few days later armed with a cassette recorder. They left food out to entice the creature and ended up capturing their first vocalizations of the beast. They were able to make several more recordings that year. These are called the Berry tapes. On one occasion, the vocalizations were accompanied by an unusual type of whistle. After several episodes of recording the rapid chatter, they once again decided that they would rush out of the shack and try to get a picture of the creatures. As soon as they were out of the shack, there was a dead silence. They thought they would hear the creatures thrashing through the brush as they ran from the hunters, but there was nothing. Just eerie silence. The hunters slowly moved toward where they had last heard the clatter. All of a sudden, they just froze in their tracks. Neither one could move. They looked at each other and said, "We need to go back!" They had no explanation for the paralyzing effect they felt. They hadn't been struck by fear when they had done this type of thing before. They could only describe it as being blocked by some type of force field.

Several years later, they were talking to a Bigfoot researcher who raised the possibility that they had been affected by infrasound, since both of them had had the same experience. This brought to mind several occasions when they had been lying in their sleeping bags hearing the beast moving around outside, but were physically unable to get up and go take a picture, as if something were holding them down. It is still not known what caused this. During the course of their investigations, they heard several strange noises. They described one as being like the sound of a tuning fork and another like a crashing metallic noise emanating from the woods. Upon investigation, however, they could find no cause for the sounds. Could this be a form of mimicry? Were the beasts copying sounds or noises that they had heard? The answer will probably never be found. One of the more disturbing sounds they encountered was a clicking noise that actually followed them home and recurred on occasion with no known cause.

The two made recordings of activity as well as vocalizations—for instance, the breaking of a branch. This sound is different from a branch falling, as it is the sharp snap of something being quickly broken. Other sounds picked up by their recorders included rocks being clapped together making a popping sound, and a large limb being hit against a boulder. These could be methods of signaling, or they could actually be an artistic expression creating a type of music. After the concert of rock-popping and limb-beating, the creatures began to whoop back and forth to each other. Singing? They could be listening to "Beast Floyd" or "Squatch Zepplin"! During the noisemaking and conversations, they always remained just out of sight, appearing only in rare fleeting glimpses.

At times, the creatures seemed to be using words, and one of the phrases caught on tape sounded like a question. It goes something like this: "Aush trol trio?" Whether the creature was trying to communicate with the hunters or another Bigfoot is unknown. Another phrase used was "Appala . . . appala?" One of the campers mimicked the sound in an attempt to elicit a reply, but there was no definite response. It seems as if the beasts were talking among themselves.

At one point, they heard what could have been a juvenile or a younger voice, which led them to conclude that this was more than likely a family unit. Even though they made no effort to conceal their noisemaking, they remained hidden. Perhaps it is all right for them to be heard but not seen. It seems that this was an instance in which the hunters were not perceived as a threat, but as a curiosity.

I believe that Bigfoots must have had some type of limited interaction with humans in order to learn about us. Know your enemy, so to speak. With limited interactions, they gather information about us that they can share with others of their kind. The noises and conversations may be intended to test human reaction. One such reaction occurred when they heard a series of whoops that the men mimicked and then, after a pause, they heard very unusual talking that they would later call "samurai chatter." This was definitely intended for other Bigfoots, possibly as a warning or instructional message. Vocalizations were recorded over several years in the area of the hunting camp, including various sounds, noises, and conversations. Several footprints were found and casts were made, varying from seven to more than eighteen inches in length, indicating a family group or various creatures.

The tapes were submitted to a number of individuals for examination, one of whom was cryptolinguist Scott Nelson. Through careful examination, he has created a Sasquatch phonetic alphabet that is formally known as the Unclassified

Hominid phonetic alphabet. This will remain its name until the animal in question has been classified by science, or until an actual existing language has been documented. We are assuming the existence of Bigfoot or Sasquatch, because the creature has to be valid in order for a language to exist. The tapes were transcribed and certain conclusions reached. The Sasquatch language, as revealed by the tapes, is uttered about twice as fast as any known human language. In order to be transcribed properly by a human ear, the tapes had to be slowed down to about half their original speed.

Since this language is of an unknown type and this is the first time it has been transcribed, the formal grammar and arrangement of words and or phrases cannot be known. The use of upper- and lowercase letters is also unknown. Sasquatch are thought to have the ability to produce vocalizations at frequencies higher or lower than those of humans, which means they should also be able to vocalize at the same frequencies as humans. They just possess a broader range of frequencies in which to communicate, which could be advantageous when communicating over distances. To go along with this, they must be able to hear these same variations of pitch and frequency.

Looking at the language from the Berry tapes, it appears that the speech was formed to make sentences. Rather than using one-word descriptives like "rock" or "tree," the ideas were expressed in multi-word phrases ranging from simple commands to complex directions. Instead of saying "go" or "stop," they appear to be saying phrases more like "You need to go" or "It's time to stop." The added wording in sentence structures elevates the sophistication of the commands or descriptions.

This, I believe, indicates higher cognitive ability. Indications are that the different forms of communication expressed in this language rise above primitive instinctive methods.

APE-SPEAK

Recordings of alleged Sasquatch vocalizations generally occur without any visual confirmation of the origin of the sounds. This makes it difficult to classify these sounds unless the recordings are of sufficiently high quality to be analyzed properly. Dr. Robert Benson of the Texas A&M Corpus Christi Center of Bioacoustics did an analysis of recordings suspected of being from a Sasquatch. The recordings were digitized for computer analysis. When a sound is generated, the teeth, tongue, pharynx, and lips act as filters to create what is known as the format structure. Animal vocalizations produce identifying format structures. Benson then used this information to rule out various animals native to the area, as well as non-native species. Once these were eliminated, he concluded that the sounds were likely primate in origin.

Dr. Gregory Bambenek, who is a clinical psychologist and avid outdoorsman, was on an investigation with a group of field researchers who were call-blasting recorded possible Sasquatch sounds hoping to elicit a response. After one blast, they heard a strange scream quite similar to the sounds they were playing. The scream was very loud and was estimated to come from a distance of about 100 yards. The volume and presence of the sound were quite incredible. Bambenek believes that whatever made the sound had to have very large lungs, probably larger than human lungs. The noise actually pushed him back against a vehicle and vibrated his pant legs and chest wall. It was like no other sound he had ever heard, definitely not from any human or any known animal. The fact that the scream vibrated his pants and chest led him to conclude that Sasquatch may use infrasounds, which cannot be heard by humans but can be felt. The infrasound was probably embedded in the scream.

One story tells of a hunter who was standing by a field when he saw a rather large deer come out of the woods into the clearing. Moments later, he heard a terrible scream. The deer froze in its tracks and a large creature walking on two legs appeared from the woods. It grabbed the deer, threw it over its shoulder, and disappeared into the brush. It could very well be that the deer was affected by infrasounds contained in the scream that prevented it from fleeing.

Many primates produce loud calls that are species-typical and that allow them to communicate over long distances. They use low-frequency calls because they are less likely to be affected by vegetation or ground reflection. Quite a few primates have inflatable air sacs that can hold up to six quarts of air. The current theory is that the air sacs are resonating chambers used to amplify vocal sounds into loud calls. The air may also be used to generate overtones that can combine with vocal sounds, possibly creating infrasounds. Some humans have an ability comparable to this, like the throat singers in Siberia, Tibet, Mongolia, and the Arctic regions. These singers combine low maintained pitches with higher pitched sounds, producing the notes by altering the shape of the vocal tract. I'm not suggesting that Bigfoots practice throat singing, but they may, perhaps, be capable of something similar.

Note, by contrast, the vocalizations made by mountain gorillas during rest and quiet feeding.

- Purr: a soft purr that sounds like a large cat.

- Soft grumble: similar to the purr, but louder and a bit harsher.

- Hum: a soft hum emitted while resting.

- Soft grunt: a series of sounds ranging from two to ten grunts, usually sounded during leisurely feeding.

- Abrupt grunts: a slow series of grunts sounding like "wo-wo-wo" that may be used to let others know the position of the dominant male.

- Bo-bo-bo call: probably used as a location call when the group is scattered.

- Neighing-horse call: self-explanatory as to the sound made, and a type of sexual attraction call.

- O-o-o-o call: forceful sound that a male uses continuously during copulation.

- Hoot: a sound usually accompanied by chest-beating.

- Yip: a call usually made before chest-beating.

- Panting ho-ho: a call given by females three times while beating their chests.

- Squeak: a call given by juveniles while chest-beating.

- Chuckle: a sound associated with infants playing.

- Harsh grunt: a sound used as a show of annoyance, both by gorillas in the wild and those in captivity.

- Bark: a noise used in conjunction with the harsh grunt to show annoyance.

The vocalizations reported by mountain gorillas don't seem to have any similarity to sounds that are attributed to Sasquatch. These are two different animals who may possibly have a very distant common ancestor, but that is where any similarity ends. Apples and oranges again.

5

Sasquatch and Remote Viewing

When I was in the woods with my sister documenting the stick structure that had changed, I took a series of pictures. There are a couple of old timers in southern Ohio who use this technique, going to places frequented by Bigfoots and just snapping a lot of pictures. They have captured a couple possible images of Bigfoot in this way. I did the same thing and caught something rather strange. There, in the leaves, was a face that looked a lot like what I imagine a Bigfoot would look like. Not an animal looking at me, but the impression of a face embedded in the fauna. I realize this is more than likely matrixing, which happens when you see a face because your mind wants to see it that way. But this picture is not leaves forming a face. It shows a face in the leaves. You can see the eyes and a nose and the distinctive crown.

Figure 12. The impression of a Bigfoot face in the leaves. Very likely matrixing, but very strange that this face appears in an area where Bigfoots are active. Native American mysticism?

The native Americans attributed mystical powers to the Sasquatch, and perhaps they were right. I think the possibility has to be raised that these creatures have some type of remote-viewing ability they use when they think they may be threatened by an intruder. There has to be some explanation for how they are able to stay so elusive and hidden, especially in places like Salt Fork, where there are so many people looking for them. Their ability to hide borders on the supernatural.

I have been a ghost hunter for a number of years and have written a book entitled *Death Explained: A Ghost Hunter's Guide to the Afterlife*. In researching for this book, I assembled an album full of ghost pictures that I intend to make into another book. Ghosts? Yes. Bigfoot? Yes. Loch Ness Monster and Jersey Devil? Probably not.

I think we need to examine as a real possibility that Bigfoot may possess something like a sixth sense. It's commonly said that animals can tell when a disaster is coming. During the tsunami that took place in Indonesia on December 26, 2004, in which hundreds of thousands of people perished, not a single animal was found among the dead. All of the local wildlife survived by moving to higher ground before the wave hit. Somehow, they knew that the disaster was imminent. Some say they felt the vibrations or felt a change in atmosphere. Whatever the explanation, they somehow knew. Not only did they know something was going to happen, but they seemed to know what, because they ran to higher ground. I contend that they did this because of a sixth sense. All animals and humans are probably born with this sense, but animals are more efficient in using it than we are. It seems that when Mother Nature sends a message, they heed it, while we tend to ignore it or don't recognize it as a warning.

CENTRAL INTELLIGENCE

In the 1970s, the Central Intelligence Agency worked with the Stanford Research Institute to develop a means of collecting accurate information concerning distant targets without actually (physically) being there. Both the Soviet Union and China were already active in using psychics and clairvoyants for espionage and information-gathering, and the CIA felt the need to attempt the same thing to counter their Cold War foes. The result was over twenty years of psychic warfare. A set of protocols were developed and a training program was begun that allowed almost anyone to offer detailed information and do it better than recognized psychics. These people could describe anything or anyone anywhere using a technique called remote viewing. The process involves selecting a general target, choosing a specific search term, directing your mental browser to a defined area, and recording all the information you access. If your general target is "dog," the information will be general. If you choose to narrow your search, you can do so by using a specific search term like "mastiff." Through the program, these people became trained psychics.

Research procols required that the search terms be kept secret in order to control the environment and eliminate imagination, in hopes of delivering the facts in a pure form. Target terms were kept confidential so there could be no outside influence from other psychic signals. These measures were put in place to keep the viewers from getting conflicting information.

Viewers were instructed not to make any assumptions about the target, no matter what evidence was available or what conclusions had been made by others. The views were performed blindly. Viewers had to relinquish all preconceptions concerning the target. If they thought they already had information about the proposed target, then the task became impossible. The part of the brain that makes assumptions can distort and contaminate the data flow. The mind doesn't like what it doesn't understand and tries to make something out of nothing. Viewers had to separate their imaginations from the task to avoid contaminating it with bad information. They had to remain focused. Try to think of this as tuning a radio, getting the right frequency, removing the static, and focusing in. All it takes is practice and training.

Next, the researchers assigned reference numbers, usually a set of two four-digit numbers that were used to further conceal the target. The numbers chosen were random numbers that represented a codename that only the project manager knew. For example, if the researcher wanted to know what happened to the submarine Kursk, which was lost by the Russian Navy in 2000, a search word would be issued using the name Kursk. The project manager would add the descriptor "final cruise," then assign reference numbers to pinpoint the target in question. When the viewers focused in on those numbers, they could connect to the target unencumbered, but were actually blind to *what* they were seeing. The numbers generated a signal that remained throughout the session. If viewers decoded the numbers, they would have uncovered the precise nature of their target. With only the target reference numbers to go on, however, their minds could open to a separate reality that sent them in the right direction to find the target.

This technique is referred to as Stage I remote viewing. It is the mechanism that allows viewers to achieve initial contact with a target. This is the foundational stage that allows us to add depth to the remote viewing effort. When achieving Stage I, you must be hyper-attentive and eliminate all distractions. The stronger your attentiveness, the stronger the signal. No matter the distance, you can zone in on the target.

Stage I consists of reaching out to a target by moving from generalized thought to a specific focus. In this stage, viewers often create or scribble a crude likeness of the target. The signal emanates from the subconscious as an impulse to the nervous system, which stimulates the hand to generate a crude image or set of jumbled and scribbled lines that contain basic data about the target. Wavy lines may represent water, while an inverted "V" may mean mountains. Jagged lines could represent lightning, a triangle could be the sail of a ship, or straight lines could be a coastline.

In Stage II remote viewing, you continue to increase your connection with the target and gather more information. You can ascertain sounds, colors, possible textures, and dimensions. In this stage, you can feel and hear everything as if you were physically there, even though you aren't. Then, in Stage III, you begin to make accurate drawings of what you observe. Your connection with the target increases with no analytical thought involved. You continue to draw what is felt and seen through your mind's eye.

In Stage IV, you receive even more information and begin to interpret the data perceived. You have a higher level of contact in which you can offer descriptive accounts or even emotional reactions to the target observed. You draw no conclusion about the target, because this is basic data reception. You can draw a precise picture or describe the location of the target at hand.

Stage V is where you break the connection and rely on memory more than perception of the target. You have enough information about the target to draw an accurate picture so what you have done pays off. Another remarkable thing is that, by using only the reference numbers, viewers can revisit the acquired target at any time. If changes occur, or if greater detail is required, this can be done rather easily.

The people the CIA trained for this type of viewing were not psychics or mediums or seers of any kind. They were just intelligent individuals who were able to make use of the natural ability it is believed we all possess. The vast majority of us don't use these techniques because we simply don't know how. It takes training and long hours of practice to master the skills. The CIA and American military do not consider this to be pseudoscience or paranormal hokum, but rather an effective, proven tool they can use to gather information.

We know that animals have demonstrated this ability, as seen during the tragic tsunami and other events. We have the ability to see remotely, too, or so it seems. If we can, then perhaps other primates can as well. The possibility of Bigfoots using this technique to remain hidden is a real possibility. Can we prove this? Probably not, but the possibility still exists. The fact that I may have caught a picture of a Bigfoot in the act of remote viewing raises questions. It is possible that quite a few Bigfoot sightings occur at night because their viewing techniques don't work well in the dark. This gives us more to think about. I am just raising questions, and not necessarily stating an argument. Because it is a woodland creature, this animal should have a psychic, spiritual, and emotional connection, along with a physical connection, to nature.

The case for remote viewing seems to be legitimate. In 1789, famed philosopher Emmanuel Swedenborg wrote in his journal that he had been terrified after witnessing, through his mind, a terrible fire in Stockholm, which was more than 300 miles away. He could offer no explanation for what he had seen. Swedenborg stated that he knew precisely where the fire started, the number of homes destroyed, and the number of people hurt in the blaze. He said he could even feel the heat from the fire. Days later, a messenger arrived with news of the fire. The vision he had seen was confirmed to the smallest detail.

The father of quantum theory, Max Planck, was aware of this phenomenon and termed it "the divine matrix," describing it as an energy field that connects all of creation. This energy field contains information. All we have to do is access it.

In 1991, Vice President Dan Quayle asked an organization named PSI Tech to find out if there were weapons of mass destruction left in Kuwait. The only other way we could possibly find out was through technological hardware and boots on the ground. If it were possible to discover and verify the location of these weapons without life being lost or resources expended, it would have been of great value. PSI Tech set up dozens of remote viewing sessions to locate any WMDs present, then analyzed all the resulting data. After reviewing their findings, they concluded that there weren't any missiles or biological agents present. Their processes confirmed that there were no WMDs in Kuwait and probably never were. One finding in particular gave them an important insight into the enemy. They saw remotely that the regular Iraqi army was a collection of forced conscripts who were half-starved outcasts thrown against coalition forces. They were afraid to cut and run for fear of reprisals against their families by Saddam Hussein and his henchmen. Once the battle took place, this was confirmed. PSI Tech also foresaw the locations of bunkers and other installations that were quickly destroyed. If the vice president had confidence enough to use this technique in a time of war, then perhaps there is something to it.

The military has now used this technique for more than twenty years. I have seen research that confirms it as valid and research that condemns it as a hoax. Either way, some humans have special abilities. In my ghost-hunting endeavors, I have run into individuals who claim to be mediums or clairvoyants. Some really have the gift, and others don't. I personally know one person who can feel the presence of a ghost and has proven it to me. The ability to reach out with the mind and obtain information exists. Whether or not it can be taught is probably another matter. The fact that some of us, as primates, have this ability leads us to reason that other primates may also have it. And if they are in tune with nature in a way that we are not, it is possible they can use this ability as a self-defense mechanism. Looking back again to the animals that survived the tsunami, there has to be some kind of awareness that can be called upon in times of danger, a sixth sense that nature has provided and most of us have lost.

6

Is Sasquatch Interdimensional?

There is a growing consensus among those in the Bigfoot community that Sasquatch is an interdimensional creature. Despite increased interest bringing more researchers into the Bigfoot woods and the use of varied and improving technologies, this creature still remains unknown. The only type of evidence that seems to present itself is blurry pictures, video clips, and occasional track casts. The use of drones, camera traps, and other ingenious methods have produced little evidence. This beast seems to be toying with us.

Native American and other cultures, both ancient and modern, attribute supernatural or mystical powers to this being. There are claims of Bigfoots being associated with UFOs and even with ghostly hauntings. The elusiveness of this animal has generated many stories and superstitions linked to the myths and legends associated with Sasquatch encounters.

In the famous story of the Ape Canyon attack of the 1920s, there is a segment that states that tracks left by the entity were found on a sandbar by a flowing creek, and that these tracks stopped in the middle of the bar as if this creature had simply disappeared leaving no tracks behind. I have cast several tracks, and each time I have found one, there has been *only* one. That is not to say that the creatures left one track and disappeared, however. It's the nature of the beast to tread on surfaces that don't easily show tracks. I believe this is a flesh-and-blood creature.

Figure 13. Fourteen-inch Bigfoot track found in eastern Ohio.

Figure 14. I cast this seventeen-inch track that my sister and I found during one of our outings.

Early humans survived by hunting in groups or tribal units. The fastest and strongest drove their prey off cliffs or used spears or other weapons to take down their quarry to feed and support other members of the tribe. Consider the Sasquatch. Indications are that they travel in family units, probably consisting of a male, a female, and one or two young. A solitary hunter, either male or female, would have to develop specialized tactics to ensure the survival of the family. In the hardwood forests of North America, the primary source of protein is prey animals that are available year-round. Being omnivorous would increase opportunities to obtain nutrition.

These prey animals would definitely include white-tail deer, as well as its cousin the mule deer. Deer can be considered nature's grocery store. They're available in ample numbers across the country in virtually every terrain. To defeat the deer's defense mechanisms and to harvest regularly, however, requires specific tactics and habits. Species that hunt deer to survive have to be masters of their environment. They have to hunt and defeat deer and other animals in all weather conditions and situations. As humans, we have never encountered anything like this.

Indeed, Sasquatches may control their world as well as we control ours. They have to be masters of stealth and cunning. I am a deer hunter and am very aware of covering or concealing my scent. Sasquatches may travel the way they do, not leaving many tracks or signs, in order to move through the forest without alarming deer in the area. A solitary Sasquatch, using stealth and cunning, controlling its environment, could easily take down a hearty meal by using its considerable upper body strength and a well-placed stone. Teaching these tactics to their young, this elusiveness and dominance of their domain, would be their way of ensuring survival. Perhaps we don't see or hear these animals because this is their lifestyle. They hide in plain sight.

It is possible that Bigfoots know us as well as they know the deer or other animals. They know how to react to us. They have watched us for centuries. I believe they know that, if one Bigfoot is sighted, we spend time in that area looking for signs of the beast or hoping for another sighting. They may use their tactics to control our search for them. We have never found where they actually live, because they don't want us intruding there. Many so-called nests have been found. I have found them myself, but I don't think these are actual habitats.

I think the nests are used as hunting blinds or storm shelters that are placed in strategic locations. These forest dwellers control every aspect of their environment. We simply don't understand them.

NO TRESPASSING

I have had interactions with at least two Sasquatch. The first time, my sister and I were revisiting an area on top of a hill where a pristine teepee structure was located. This structure was well-maintained and, over time, the sticks and logs were rearranged to create subtle changes that I believe to be messages that were changed or updated as the structure was changed (see Figures 3 and 4 on page 35).

When we arrived at the base of the hill, we noticed that a broken tree had been placed across the trail as a barrier. In fact, there were two of them. We hesitated, but decided to climb the hill anyway. When we crossed the barriers, there was a loud knocking noise. This was in early fall and I tried to determine if this could have been an acorn or walnut falling. But there was no subsequent sound of anything bouncing or rolling, and the noise was too loud and close to be a branch falling or any other possible natural occurrence. My thoughts turned to a possible tree knock, but there was no movement or any other sound. If something was that close and made a tree knock, I would have seen something or heard additional sounds.

As a deer hunter, I have trained myself to notice any movement in the woods. I hone in on any motion—the flick of a tail, a squirrel scampering, birds fluttering, etc. Any movement could be a deer moving in and this gives me time to react. In this instance, when I heard the knocking sound, I was just as attuned to my surroundings as if I were on a deer hunt, and there was nothing. No sounds. No movement. Nothing to indicate that anything was there. This could not have been a tree knock, because there was absolutely no movement.

I concluded that it was a loud click or knocking sound made by something flicking its tongue. I can mimic the sound, but not nearly as loudly as what I heard that day. I think the sound was made to alert anything on top of the hill that we were climbing up. I believe there were Squatches in them thar woods.

The second encounter occurred in the month of March, when my sister and I were walking a trail where some pine-tree arches were located. I tend to drag my sister around the Bigfoot woods. The trail we were walking was flanked on each side by thick brush and briars. Along the trail, we found what looked like a juvenile track. It wasn't deep enough to cast, so I took a picture of it with my sister's booted foot in the frame to give a sense of scale.

As we walked the trail looking for more tracks or other evidence, we heard a turkey yelping fairly close to where we were. The brush was too thick to see the turkey, but it was rather close. As an experienced turkey hunter as well as a deer hunter, I was rather excited to be this close to one, even if it wasn't in season. I wasn't armed anyway. As we walked along, the turkey seemed to be traveling parallel to us, but out of sight. This went on for about ten minutes and then we both heard a short, sharp growl. Again, this was close by—perhaps no more than thirty feet away. Keep in mind that the cover was still too thick to see into the surrounding woods.

We heard this growl twice. We stopped and listened quietly for any other sounds. There is nothing in the Ohio woods that growls like this. We have deer and raccoons and other woodland creatures, but nothing that makes such a defined growl. I thought that perhaps it could be an old farm dog chasing rabbits, or even a coyote, but there was no noise of anything moving through the brush or any other animal noise, like barking or howling. No noise.

After thinking about it a bit, I concluded that perhaps we had interrupted a Sasquatch stalking the turkey and it was letting us know it. We walked the trail a little farther to a spot where the brush opens up to the woods and watched as the turkey came into view. Not wanting to spook it, we turned and walked back down the trail. I returned to that spot later that summer and, in the place where the turkey had exited the brush into the forest, there was a new stick structure. I think the resident Squatch was letting me know that this was his turf. I now respect its territory.

OTHER WORLDS

So, why do we think that anything could be interdimensional? Alternate universes were proposed to explain peculiarities in quantum mechanics and string theory. Without them, the eleven dimensions of particle physics fail to materialize. Proponents of a multiverse suggest that there are an infinite number of parallel universes. Einstein contended that these universes would mirror our own. Under his theory, there are infinite versions of you and me living every conceivable existence, each alternate existence obeying its own laws of physics.

In my book *Death Explained*, I present a theory that, when we pass, we enter a parallel universe, or another dimension, that allows for the existence of energy beings. I believe this is what we become after we leave our bodies when we die. We transform and exist in time, unlike our existence in this dimension, which is rooted in space. We go from space-time to time-space. As energy-based lifeforms, we can travel between that existence and this one. When we interact with this existence as an energy being, they call it a haunting. Being from here and ending up there, with occasional interactions, we are interdimensional once we pass. Since we can interact, and there are most likely an infinite number of other universes, then it stands to reason that these interactions have taken place throughout human history.

Persistent stories of strange creatures and apparitions have always been considered folklore or myth or superstition. Many ancient cultures have depicted half-human, half-animal beasts that we interpret as gods or religious representations. In medieval times, there were tales of werewolves and dragons. In the epic *Beowulf*, Grendel seems to resemble a Sasquatch. In Biblical times, stories of giants and angels that interact to guide us or treat us with malice are common. Ancient alien enthusiasts believe that humanity was guided and assisted by beings from another dimension or some distant planet.

Much of today's science relies on its conclusions being either observable or predictable using mathematics. The thought of interdimensional interaction by strange lifeforms is tucked away in the realm of superstition and the paranormal, too outlandish to be considered. This is not correct; it is incomplete. After amassing considerable evidence for the existence of ghosts, Sasquatch, and probable multiverse interactions, I could tell these scientists a thing or two.

One of the most famous, or infamous, interactions with a possible interdimensional creature is the story of the Mothman of Point Pleasant, West Virginia. On November 12, 1966, a group of workers were digging a grave near Clendenin, West Virginia. These workers reported seeing a human-like figure flying from nearby trees over their heads. This was the first report of this unknown creature.

A few days later, on November 15, two teenage couples from Point Pleasant reported to local police that they had witnessed a large creature with red, glowing eyes and ten-foot wings flying around and following their car near the site of a World War II munitions plant that was referred to locally as the TNT.

During the next few days, other sightings of this being were reported. Among them were reports by two volunteer firemen who described the creature as a large bird with bright red eyes. A contractor told a local sheriff that he had seen the figure in a field and, when he pointed a flashlight at it, the eyes shone like bicycle reflectors. A wildlife biologist told reporters that he thought this could be a sandhill crane, a large bird not native to the area. I have seen sandhill cranes and personally don't think they inspire that kind of fear.

Whatever this creature was, it made a lasting impression on those who witnessed it. After the Silver Bridge tragedy of

December 15, 1967, the Mothman creature was considered a harbinger of disaster and was the subject of *The Mothman Prophecies,* a 1975 book and later a 2002 movie starring Richard Gere.

The legend has had a lasting impact on Point Pleasant. A twelve-foot metal sculpture of the Mothman was erected in the town square in 2003, and the town has an annual Mothman Festival each fall. The Mothman has become something of a cottage industry for the small, rural town, with a variety of merchandise available in assorted shops along the main drag. There is a Mothman museum and a Mothman diner where they serve a very tasty "Mothman Burger"—not made of actual Mothman, I have been assured.

So several people reported seeing a large bird-like creature with red, glowing eyes flying around. The town cashes in on it with festivals and attractions. So what? What's the big deal? I heard the stories and watched the shows on TV and didn't think much about it, since there is nothing in the fossil records to indicate there was ever a flying humanoid. And besides, they say it's probably just a large bird.

In February 2016, my sister and I decided to go to Mothman territory just to say we had been there. The weather wasn't too bad for late winter, cool and overcast with occasional drizzle. We stayed in a motel in Portsmouth, Ohio, across the Ohio River not far from Point Pleasant, and drove across into West Virginia. We did the usual, going to the Mothman museum and eating at the diner, whose owner actually had had a Mothman experience.

While we were at the museum, I bought a map of the McClintic Wildlife Management Area, which was one of the areas known as the TNT. We drove to the area famous for the Mothman sightings and, in one spot, we noticed some deer carcasses. We counted nine skeletons in a fairly small area. Some of the remains looked fairly fresh, since the bones were still red. These animals had been devoured. As a deer hunter, I have seen several instances of poachers killing and stripping carcasses, but not on this scale. I know it wasn't coyotes, because it's not typical behavior for them to drag so many deer to a feeding area. If the deer had been downed by coyotes, it would have to have been a large pack attacking an entire herd. This was February, so there was no open hunting season and this was in a wildlife management area that was protected. I don't think any official would dump roadkill deer there, and the road is too rough to go fast enough to hit and kill one deer, not to mention nine. The deer carcasses are a mystery. My impression was that this was a deliberate feeding area for something.

As we drove around, we passed a car with Ohio plates and stopped to talk to the driver, a girl from Akron who was in Point Pleasant for a family birthday party. Since she was in the area, she decided to check out the TNT. We were looking for the bunkers and she thought she might know where they were. We did end up finding some, and my sister and I asked her if she would take a picture of us in front of one. She did so, but told us that she didn't think it would turn out because of the light. I didn't think much about it. It was a dreary, overcast day and I, too, thought there probably wasn't enough light. We went into the bunker and I took some pictures on the inside, but didn't notice anything out of the ordinary.

When I got home, I put the camera's SD card into my computer to look at the pictures we had taken. When the picture the girl took (unfortunately, I can't recall her name) came up on the screen, I saw what she had meant by the light. Both my head and my sister's were bathed in light. Even stranger, there appeared to be a very tall misty figure standing in the doorway behind us. This figure had to be at least ten feet tall. Could this be Mothman manifesting behind us? We will never know. It certainly was strange to go to this location and encounter a large, unknown form where Mothman was supposed to be.

I think it is possible that a portal opened above us that created this light, which we did not see, but the camera did. Once this portal opened, an interaction occurred with an interdimensional entity, possibly a Mothman-type creature or something else. We did not see, hear, or feel anything out of the ordinary, which leads me to believe this was occurring outside of our perceived reality.

Why would I think that something as exotic as an interdimensional portal could even exist? Because I have encountered at least one before. The more I investigate and the deeper I get into paranormal phenomena, the stranger my world gets. I'm having the time of my life.

THINGS THAT GO
BUMP IN THE NIGHT

My wife and I went to a coworker's house in Cardington, Ohio, where the couple were experiencing episodes of paranormal activity. The wife reported hearing strange noises and seeing fleeting glimpses of shadows darting about. The focal point of the experiences was a bathroom area adjacent to their bedroom. She had taken a picture in the bathroom mirror and captured the figure of a man wearing a hat in the room behind her. I asked questions about the possible haunting to try to determine if it was a simple human spirit running about. There were no reports of objects being thrown or any scratches or bodily attacks occurring. I make it a point to avoid anything that might be demonic in nature.

When we arrived at the house, we sat around the kitchen table, where I showed them my ghost-picture album. From the kitchen table, I had a view of their laundry room, where I actually saw a small ball of light hovering. I had my special cameras with me (full-spectrum and night-vision) and I took a picture with my night-vision camera set to daytime mode. What I caught looked like a wave, comparable to a wave in a pond, moving from the laundry room and into the living room. The wave, shaped like a bow, extended from ceiling to floor like a sonic boom. I did not see the bow effect with my eyes, only with my camera.

After this, I went around the house taking random pictures. I didn't catch anything else until I went into the bathroom off the bedroom. There were no windows in this room, so I went in alone and in the dark. I was using my night-vision camera in nighttime mode. I took a picture in the mirror to see if I could catch the figure wearing the hat, then I turned into the room taking random shots. I did not see or hear anything. I didn't have any feelings of dread or anything like that, because I am not at all sensitive to that type of thing. I took more pictures in the bedroom and finished our investigation.

I once asked Kris Williams (from the *Ghost Hunters* TV program) during an investigation at the Morrison Lodge in Elizabethtown, Kentucky, why they investigated at night. She said it was to keep contamination down. I prefer to investigate during the day and do quite well.

Once I got home and plugged the camera's SD card into my computer, I saw the bow effect in the living room and was totally amazed to see what I would call a sunburst in the pictures from the bathroom. The pictures I took in the mirror showed a light with beams emanating from the edges. I aimed my night-vision camera at the mirror in my home and got the same effect. The strange thing was that, in the picture taken in the mirror in the haunted bathroom, there are baffling things coming out of the sunburst of light. At the top of this light is a figure that looks like a face and head. This could be a reflection or flare, but on the bottom, there is a strange doll-like arm coming out of the sphere. You can even see fingers. I thought there might be a doll or toy in the frame to give this effect, but there was nothing there.

In the next picture, which was taken directly into the bathroom, the starburst is still there and there is a large black arm-like feature blocking the molding and wall below the light. I cannot even venture a guess as to the physics of this event, but I believe I captured an interdimensional portal. Whether these are ghosts or some other incredible beings from a parallel universe, I can only guess. After this experience, the opening of a portal above us at the TNT and illuminating us and depositing an entity behind us is not out of the realm of possibility.

Another possible interdimensional event happened at the Ohio State Reformatory in Mansfield, Ohio. This prison was built between 1886 and 1910 and remained open until 1990, when it was closed by court order. The Ohio Reformatory Preservation Society promotes events to generate funds for construction projects, including public ghost hunts. My wife, Vicki, and I go every year, and I usually catch something anomalous, from energy streaks to full-bodied apparitions. This is probably the most haunted place we have ever visited.

On one of these ghost hunts, I was in the library taking pictures with my night-vision camera and caught something strange in one of the windows. This library is on the second floor, so there couldn't have been anyone standing outside of the window. Moreover, the windows were covered with black plastic sheeting. I caught the figure of a man in some type of Victorian clothing, floating as if he were in the distance. I estimated the window was about twelve feet from where I was standing, but the figure seemed farther away, as if in another reality. I went back and took a picture of the same window, but the figure was gone. I have a before and after for comparison. Who this figure was, and where it was, will remain a mystery.

The first full-bodied apparition that I ever captured on camera also came from Mansfield the first time that my wife and I attended an overnight public ghost hunt at the Reformatory. We were using disposable 35mm cameras that I had picked up at Walgreens. I think we had four or five of them, or about a hundred pictures. I had an EMF detector with me that I had bought on eBay and I snapped a picture whenever the meter spiked. I didn't realize until later investigations that wiring and conduits could set the meter off.

We took pictures here and there around the prison, including several in the Bullpen, a huge central area from which you can access the different cell blocks. When they have these public ghost hunts, the prison staff orders pizza around 10:30 or 11 PM, so everyone can take a break and exchange stories about what they have or haven't found. We enjoyed pizza and drinks with everyone else and thought that we had hit the building pretty hard, so we decided to go back to our motel and get some sleep.

While standing on the landing leading down to the Bullpen, my wife discovered that she had one picture left in her camera, so she just pointed it toward the north cell block and took one final shot. When we got the film developed, it turned out that this last picture caught an apparition that seemed to be wearing Victorian clothing and was possibly sitting in a wheelchair. I took the picture back at a later date and found that the figure seemed to be floating about three feet off the floor. I was very proud of this picture and I showed it to everyone who had an interest.

Recently, I ran across the pictures from this adventure and noticed something quite extraordinary. I found another picture taken from about the same angle in the Bullpen, but without the ghost figure. The ghost picture showed a pillar, a white sign, and a pylon in the background, as did the picture without the entity. In the pre-ghost photo, the sign mounted on the closest pillar reads "Bullpen." In the ghost picture, there is no sign on the pillar or any indication that a sign was ever there. Another picture taken in the same area, but from a different angle, shows a sign or plaque hung beside a large doorway that also doesn't appear in the ghost picture. I have pictures of this same area showing subtle differences, but the most startling difference is the addition of the ghost. Could I have taken a picture of another reality or dimension created by the energy of the ghost, or a possible portal? I can't say for sure, but something strange was created by this entity. In my book *Death Explained*, I present a theory that, as energy beings, we exist in time as opposed to existing in space, as we do in this life. This could be a picture taken in a time before the signs were put up. Creepy!

The point I am making is that other dimensions or parallel universes may exist, and I have actually experienced interactions that seem to be more normal than paranormal. If I can experience this much activity, then it must happen quite often. It may be that we just don't have the ability to observe it without special equipment. Bigfoot may or may not be interdimensional, and other cryptids may fit into this category as well. I am considering writing another book on the subject, since there seems to be much interest in this field. We need to make others aware of this phenomenon, because it could explain so much once we understand what is going on. Even though so-called legitimate science will make every effort to ignore and discredit these phenomena, we must bring them to light because they are part of our natural world, as well as other worlds.

To think that our home planet is the only one that could support interdimensional activity is incorrect. The universe is infinite and has always existed. Moreover, there are an infinite number of universes. Our so-called "big bang" is only one of countless big bangs going on all the time. We just are not aware of them. I believe that life has always existed. There was never a beginning. Life moves from one parallel universe to another through portals or wormholes connecting them.

Each universe has its own set of physical laws that dictates the type and variety of life it contains. In our reality, our physical laws allow for organic life that becomes an energy form once physical bodies are discarded. As energy forms, we enter another dimension where the physical laws allow us to continue our existence in time-space. Einstein said that parallel universes mirror each other and are connected by a sort of quantum entanglement. Life did not start in a mud puddle or some volcanic vent. Consciousness and an eternal spirit are not chemical reactions. We are matter-energy hybrids.

ENIGMATIC VISITORS

Some hold that life came here from outer space. This theory is called "panspermia." But within this theory, the same problem exists. Where in the solar system did life magically appear if it was sent here on a meteor or comet? It may be that life came here on an interstellar comet, but, so far, we haven't seen any proof of this.

Stories of strange and unusual creatures are peppered throughout human history. There has never been a shortage of theories about these entities. Here are a couple of stories about unknown creatures that seem to fit the description of interdimensional beings. For instance, there is no evidence for them in the fossil record, they are only sighted for brief periods of time, and there are no reports of similar creatures. Even if we accept that other creatures that come from a parallel universe may be seen from time to time, these creatures still seem totally out of place.

In the fall of 1903, residents in the town of Van Meter, Iowa, encountered a fantastic beast that came to be known as the Van Meter Visitor. This animal was thought to have emerged from an old mine located nearby. It was described as a bat-like humanoid with large wings and a horn on top of its head that contained a bright light. Wherever this creature came from, it must have adapted to hunt in total darkness. Drawings produced of the creature show it as a form of pterodactyl from some far-off world. This creature was seen by the town doctor and a bank cashier named Peter Dunn. Mr. Dunn cast a huge footprint of the beast, which had three toes. Several attempts were made to shoot the creature, some by those who were regarded as excellent shots, but no one could bring it down. Eventually, the townspeople chased it back into the old mine and it was never seen again. Since this event has several witnesses and a print cast, it is probable that it actually happened. Where the creature came from and where it went remain a mystery.

In the town of Loveland, Ohio, what I consider to be the strangest of sightings occurred. In May 1955, a businessman was driving along the Miami River near the Branch Hill neighborhood when he noticed a group of three toad-like creatures standing by a bridge. They were three or four feet tall, bipedal, and weighed approximately fifty pounds. This gentleman noticed that they had wrinkles on their heads instead of hair. What really startled him was that one of the frogmen waved a wand-like object over its head that spewed sparks from the end. The experience proved to be too much for this poor soul and he ran for the hills. In 1972, a police officer saw another lizard-like creature near the same area, but he was sure that this was actually an escaped iguana or someone's pet and not what had come to be called the "Loveland Frog."

Not all interdimensional visitors need to be monsters or strange beasts. Take, for instance, the story of the Green Children of Woolpit, which dates from the 12th century outside of a farming community in England. Two children, a brother and sister, were found by reapers wandering near the field in which they were working. They wore strange clothing made of unfamiliar material and had skin with a green hue. They spoke in a language that was unintelligible to the local people. The children were taken to the village and eventually taken into the home of Sir Richard de Calne at Wilkes. The foundlings appeared to be starving, but refused to eat until presented with beans, which they ate heartily. They ate mostly beans until they developed a taste for bread. The boy became ill and soon died, but the girl survived, eventually losing the green tint of her skin. She grew up and married an Englishman, and told the story of herself and her brother once she learned to speak English.

She claimed that she and her brother had been tending their father's flock in a land called the Land of St. Martin, where there was perpetual twilight. The people who dwelled in this land all had green-tinted skin. She also spoke of a luminous land across a river. The children wandered into a cave and became hopelessly lost. They finally exited the labyrinth to be found by the English villagers. This account was recorded by Ralph of Coggeshall in the *Chronicum Anglicanum*. It was also recorded by William of Newburgh in the *Historia rerum Anglicarum*. There is a sign at the entrance to the village of Woolpit depicting the children.

We must remember that the doorway between dimensions swings both ways. There are numerous accounts of people vanishing without a trace, like the unfortunate young man who entered the Ugly Tuna Saloon near the Ohio State University campus in the late 1970s and was never seen again. Security cameras show him entering, but never exiting. Did he pass into another dimension? He is the only one who knows. Humans who pass through interdimensional portals may be seen as strange monsters and beasts by inhabitants on the other side who don't know what a human is. To them, we may be the fantastic creatures that no one believes are real.

I truly believe that the Bigfoots residing in the forests of North America and elsewhere are flesh and blood and are indigenous to this reality. My sister and I once walked a dry creek bed in an active area. We stopped for a bit, looking for Bigfoot evidence, and I took a number of random pictures into the surrounding woods. When I examined the photos on my computer, I found that I had caught four of the creatures hunkered down in the brush, watching what we were doing! It took me a moment to realize that I had actual Bigfoot pictures, and that I was the one who took them. Thus I have evolved from a believer to a knower. I had been in this area before and found evidence like tracks and structures. When I combined this with the knowledge I had of the terrain and flora of the area, I realized there is no reason to assume these figures were anything other than Sasquatch inhabiting this forest. These creatures are real, without a doubt!

I heard no noise, sensed no smell, saw no movement. The creatures were hiding in plain sight. There have never been any reports or indications that there could be, or ever was, an interdimensional portal in this area, so I am sure these cryptids were local.

On the other hand, just because we have earthly Bigfoots doesn't mean that there aren't interdimensional versions of this type of creature. According to physicists, all possibilities exist. The green children of Woolpit seemed very human, but

Figure 15. Guardian Bigfoot on the lookout for trespassers.

emerged from what may have been a parallel reality. Indeed, it is probable that there are many versions of humans, as well as versions of other creatures like Sasquatch, existing in many different realities that interact with this world, most notably at a place called the Skinwalker Ranch.

THE SKINWALKER
AND THE WITCH

There is an area in northeast Utah where incredible paranormal activity has been reported over a long period time. This area, known as the Skinwalker Ranch, is believed to be the location of an interdimensional portal. There have been reports of a Bigfoot type creature coming out of this portal.

As I researched the events that have occurred at the Skinwalker Ranch, it seemed that some of the phenomena reported at this location sounded familiar. I had encountered this somewhere before. Then I remembered that similar events had been experienced by a family in Adams, Tennessee, over 200 years ago. They called this haunting the Bell Witch.

One of the first encounters at the Skinwalker Ranch involved the appearance of an unusually large wolf. The beast appeared docile at first, but then attacked some of livestock, causing the family living there to attempt to kill it. Several shots hit the beast to no avail. As they followed the devil wolf, its tracks ended as if it had just vanished, leaving no additional sign.

The Bell Witch tale likewise begins with the sighting of strange animals around the homestead. One was reported to be a dog with a rabbit head. When a local resident encountered the strange beast, he took a shot at it and it simply disappeared.

At the Skinwalker Ranch, the wolf incident led to more strange activity. (It was later learned that there were almost no wolves in the area, with the last reported wolf shot in 1929.) Ellen, who lived at the ranch with her husband, Tom, began to question her sanity. Kitchen utensils went missing and later turned up in strange places. These odd occurrences happened a couple of times a week. Tom was bewildered when a heavy post-hole digger went missing when he knew exactly where he had left it. Other tools disappeared, only to turn up somewhere else.

At the Bell cabin, the unusual activity included sugar being taken from bowls, milk spilling for no reason, and quilts disappearing from the beds. This seemed to be classic poltergeist activity.

At the Skinwalker Ranch, when Tom and his nephew Dave went on a nighttime jaunt to check on the cows, Tom saw the lights of what he thought was an RV in the distance. He was concerned, because he really didn't like trespassers. As they watched what they interpreted to be headlights and taillights, the vehicle appeared to approach a fence line. Not wanting to repair any fencing, the pair started running toward the interlopers. They were amazed as the source of the lights began to levitate over the fence and above the trees. As the strange craft hung silhouetted against the sky, they could see it was not an RV, but an oblong object that disappeared into the darkness. They believed this could have been a UFO.

On the Bell farm, strange lights were also reported in the fields. They referred to them as flickering candles. The strange lights are still reported to this day. There was a sighting of what some called an upside-down kettle. Could they possibly be referring to a UFO?

A team from the National Institute for Discovery Science, or NIDS, investigated the strange occurrences at the Skinwalker Ranch. The team consisted of researchers from various fields. While watching from a bluff one evening, team members saw a strange yellow light appear. This glowing anomaly grew and morphed into a tunnel. One of the crew watched the spectacle through binoculars and, to his amazement, a large faceless black humanoid exited the tunnel and lumbered away. The creature seemed reminiscent of a Sasquatch. The tunnel then dissipated as if it had never been there, leaving the creature in the night with the shaken investigators. Once they gathered their senses, the team looked for sign of the apparition to no avail. Another brick in the paranormal wall.

History shows that Native American superstitions were associated with both the Skinwalker and Bell Witch locations. At the Utah ranch, a legend concerning the Ute and Navajo tribes that dates from the mid-1800s tells how Utes engaged in the slave trade, abducting Navajos and others, then selling them in the slave markets of New Mexico. During the Civil War, Ute raiders embarked on military campaigns against the Navajos. It is believed that the Navajos put a curse on the Utes, inflicting a skinwalker, or shape-shifting witch, upon them. The ranch is located on sacred ground thought to lie in the path of the skinwalker.

At the Bell farm in Tennessee, there is a cave with a natural spring running through it in which the Bell Witch is rumoured to reside. This became known as the Bell Witch Cave. One of the large rooms inside the cave contains a Native American burial. Sometime in the past, the skeleton of the Native American in the burial pit was stolen. Its whereabouts are still unknown. Directly above the cave is a Native American cemetery that is considered sacred ground. Some are convinced that disturbing these burials caused the strange activity on the Bell's property.

Something was going on at the Skinwalker Ranch, however, that was never associated with activity at the Bell farm, something that is usually not associated with hauntings or poltergeist activity. There were continuing occurrences of cattle mutilation. Although sometimes connected to UFO activity, this kind of attack is not usually encountered in reports of possible ghosts or interdimensional manifestations.

The Dugway Proving Ground, located in western Utah, has come to be known as Area 52. This installation was built in the early 1940s as a place to develop and test chemical, biological, and radiological weapons. This is where napalm was developed. This compound reportedly has underground facilities that are rumored to contain UFO technology, either developed there or reverse-engineered from UFO crashes. In March 1968, at a location near Skull Valley, Utah, a suspected nerve agent was released, killing over 6000 sheep. Since the Skinwalker Ranch is down-range or down-wind of this location, some think that the cattle mutilations were conducted by the government to monitor possible contamination from chemical or biological weapons testing and that they were done in this way to camouflage this activity.

Several remote viewing sessions were conducted to try to determine the cause of events happening at the Skinwalker Ranch. The first identified locations and landmarks that were unknown to the viewer. The second determined that the homestead was the focal point of most of the activity. The third sensed that a robotic drone was responsible for the cattle mutilations—possibly interdimensional, but connected to the military. The fourth viewing also connected the military to events at the ranch.

The military could be responsible for the cattle mutilations and at least some of the UFO sightings at the Skinwalker Ranch, but that leaves us with questions about the rest of the events that happened there.

It is quite possible that interdimensional portals were opened at both the Skinwalker Ranch and the Bell farm that released various entities and ghostly beings. Portals like these probably go back to antiquity.

As my pictures of a starburst portal with something strange coming out of it prove, portals are real, and interactions between realities occur. Until we know the physics behind these interactions, however, they will remain in the realm of the paranormal and superstition. Human hauntings usually have a history associated with them. Aunt Gertrude passed away and now she haunts the upstairs bedroom, for example. These human ghosts usually leave subtle hints that they are there so you won't be frightened. They are usually reclusive, staying in the least-used parts of the dwelling. No big deal. We get used to them.

Interdimensional creatures, on the other hand, seem to come and go, entering and exiting through portals. Some are just passing through, many are not aware of us or our surroundings. Some are Bigfoot-type creatures, some are human-like. The ones that wreak havoc and are mischievous, like those at the Skinwalker Ranch or the Bell farm, present the greatest mystery.

7

Native Legends of the Hairy Man

When we examine some of the stories or myths from Native American cultures, mainly in the Pacific Northwest, we get the idea that they really were trying to make sense out of or rationalize something real that they did not understand.

The Kwaguilth culture of British Columbia tells of a hair-covered female giant called the D'sonoqua who lives in the coastal forests and is supposed to be nocturnal. Her face is described as dark, with protruding brow ridges, dark eyes, and large ape-like lips. The D'sonoqua are said to be very stout, about twice the size of a human, with large hairy hands. The female has large hanging breasts similar to the creature seen walking through the northern California forest in the famous Patterson-Gimlin film (see chapter 10). They are strong enough to tear down trees and travel underground, perhaps explaining why they are so elusive. They speak very loudly in a language dominated by the "H" sound and communicate by whistling. They are believed to carry off young children and steal salmon from the village. Imagine the horror of being a child in one of these tribes and being constantly fearful that a monster will carry you off.

Similar tales are told about the Buk'ws, or wild man, who was said to be the model for carved wooden masks showing ape-like features, with deep-set eyes, protruding brow ridges, and an abundance of thick hair. The wild man appears at night and disappears during the day. It is not a threat to man and is said to have the ability to move great distances in an instant. When it runs, it has a stride several times that of a man. It has the habit of pounding on trees with a stick, similar to many reports of Sasquatch behavior. The Buk'ws are known in other tribal areas as Bu'oogh or Ba'wes. These names translate to something like "ape," or "monkey," or anything that imitates man. The stories tell of a creature a bit more intelligent than an ape, however, something that lives without the benefit of tech-nology, human shelter, or tools, depending more on sticks and rocks and what nature provides.

In one account, a native went to a small island on a hunting trip. He had set up his camp above the beach and built a fire to settle in for the night. As he sat there, something huge began throwing pinecones at him. This continued for a while, until he remembered what legend said you were supposed to do if you ever encountered the beast. The story goes that, if you ignore the creature, it will eventually go away. So he sat there paying no attention to what was going on and the pinecones stopped coming. He figured the animal had gotten bored and left. After this encounter, he was very wary when he went on his hunt, but the creature never returned.

On Vancouver Island, they call the hair-covered humanoid creatures Mai-a-tlatl. One legend tells of a group of Native Americans who were traveling across what is known as the Forbidden Plateau in the 1800s. The men of the tribe had encountered another tribe and told their women and children to stay on the plateau. After the encounter, they went to retrieve their families and found that they were gone. Legend has it that they were carried away by the mountain giants. It's possible, of course, that the other tribe found them, but that's not how the story goes.

Native peoples living in Nanaimo have a tradition that there are actually three types of Sasquatch. Two are said to be somewhat larger than a man, black and covered with hair. These are named Squee'noos and Papay'oos. They are woodland creatures with no special powers and can be seen from time to time. It is said that, if you can get one of these as a guardian spirit, it will make you stronger. On the down side, it will also make you unlucky. The third type is a tree-striker known as the Kwai-a-tiatl. This creature is similar to the other two but is known to knock down trees and make lots of noise. If you try to follow its tracks, it is said that it will drive you crazy. The Kwai-a-tiatl is suspected of abducting women. There are stories of abducted women having strange children after being taken and the children perishing soon after birth.

A SQUATCH BY ANY OTHER NAME

The actual name Sasquatch comes to us from the coastal Salish language. Their word for the creature is "suhsq'uhtch."

These creatures usually appear alone and are described as men about eight feet tall covered with fur. They leave large foot-prints, some as long as twenty inches. Legend states that their touch can render you unconscious. They are also reported to abduct women who then bear half-human children. They are reputed to have some form of language that they teach to the abducted women.

Another variation on the Sasquatch name comes from the same area. This goes back to when there were no white men and only native tribes in the coastal region. The male animal is called Sesq'ec and the female is Qulelitl. They are described as being very big and tall and resembling people. The Qulelitl are believed to be the wives of the Sesq'ec, so the tribes obviously believed there was some type of social order among the creatures.

In the Lummi area of coastal British Columbia, there are tales of a great tall animal called the C'amek'wes, which is said to reside in the mountains. It is man-like in shape, shaggy like a bear, and stands over seven feet tall. They appear to have left the region when the white settlers arrived. The natives considered the creature to be very wise and they never attempted to kill it. They believed that, if you saw one, it could make you crazy. The C'amek'wes make whistling noises instead of talking.

Inhabitants of the west coast of Vancouver Island believed that a hairy giant lived there in the mountains. They called this giant Matlox and it was said to be an unspeakable terror with a monstrous body covered with black hair and a head like that of a human with large eyes and teeth. It had a fierce howl and large arms, and its fingers and toes had large curved nails. It could smash you to pieces with a single blow. The natives are very familiar with bears, with Vancouver Island having a large population of them, but this narrative describes something very different and fearsome, and unknown. It was best to avoid encountering this creature at all costs.

In northern Washington state lives the Twana tribe. Some of their beliefs contain stories of mountain and forest giants called Ciatqo. The translation of this is something like stick Indians, with the term stick referring to forest. They have a human-like form, are taller than ordinary men, and live in the rough forests and foothills of mountains. They can climb vertical cliffs and leap great distances. They are rumored to be invisible and can walk up on game without being noticed. They are feared because they represented something unknown rather than a perceived threat.

In British Columbia, the Bella Coda tribe tells stories of a hairy human-like beast called the Boq, or wild man of the woods. The tribe makes masks depicting the wild man that show some with hooked noses and wide nostrils, and some with flat nostrils that appear to be ape-like. Some appear to represent females. There's a story about a young man and his family who were camping near the territory where the wild man was said to live. One evening, they heard a number of the beasts in the woods not far from them. The young man got his gun and started yelling for them to go away, because he feared for his family. He could hear the breaking of branches and pounding on tree trunks as the wild men approached. As they grew nearer, he fired his gun in their direction. The result was intense grunting and more pounding and breaking of branches. He gathered up his family and they hurriedly set out in their canoe. They heard the beasts thrashing about and saw vague outlines on the beach they had just left. The creatures did not follow the family, but it was a tense situation nonetheless.

On another occasion, a tribal chief was traveling overland and stopped along a secluded bay to pick up some shellfish. He noticed a large hairy wild man in the distance doing the same thing. He decided that he would attack the creature and take the shellfish from him. As the creature made piles of the fresh catch, the chief raised his musket and fired upon the animal. To his disbelief, the gun exploded in his hands without injuring him. He attributed this to mystical powers possessed by the Boqs and made a hasty retreat.

There is a population of Boqs reported on King Island off the coast of British Columbia. Legend states that, when the white man arrived, all the supernatural creatures fled except for the giants of the forest, who remained hidden. They stay to themselves, foraging for food, and are heard knocking on trees. When encountered, they exhibit aggressive vocal behavior.

Another variation of the creatures, the Atlakw's, are believed to have lived as humans did in the distant past, making fire and using tools. Following a war between the Atlakw's and neighboring tribes, the Atlakw's were driven deeper into the woods, where they lost their human traits and grew hair all over their bodies. Although few in number, they are said to still inhabit the wilderness. This group could, however, be a relic population of ancient humans and not actual Sasquatches, since they use fire and tools.

The Heiltsuk people of British Columbia called the wild man of the woods Pkw's. They also make ornamental masks that have deep-set eyes and rows of teeth depicting this terrible creature. One story tells of a female Pkw's who carries a basket on her back and steals children to put in it. She reportedly took a young boy from a village and kept him for a year. One day, while the Pkw's was gathering clams, the boy was told by another to gather clams and put them on his fingers and make a clapping sound with them. The beast asked him to stop and ran away, falling off a cliff to its death. Sounds like a story told to keep the kids in line. "Do this or the Pkw's will get you!"

The Tlinget of southeast Alaska tell of a hair-covered, human-like beings called Kushtakaas, who are thought to be revenants of lost relatives. They believe these creatures were somehow lost from their kind and transformed into something like land otters, growing hair all over their bodies and losing the power of reason. They then bonded with other lost souls. They subsist on shellfish and other aquatic creatures along the rocky shores and whistle to communicate, just as otters do. Sometimes they make a sound like that of a crying baby. They are feared because they can take your soul through some kind of hypnosis. It is forbidden to kill a Kushtakaas, however, because it could be someone's lost relative.

There's a strong tradition of leaving these wild men alone, and the tribe does not condone anyone attempting to shoot one. There are various stories about this creature following hunters and mimicking them, as well as reports of them throwing rocks and pinecones at individuals and making crying noises in the distance. They transform themselves into human shape to lure humans into the forest so they can hypnotize them and take their souls, making their victims one of their own kind. The land otter people are considered to be supernatural.

There are also stories of another type of wild man living nearby called Hootsland, which translates to "bear man." This is a hairy human-like monster that lives in the brush and more closely resembles what we know as a Sasquatch. Apparently, native people can tell the difference between the two, but I think I would be a bit confused.

Another group named the Haida, who reside on Prince of Wales Island off the southern coast of Alaska, have a similar story about lost or confused natives becoming wild men. For some reason, this has become a recurring theme offered to explain the human-like beings running around in the woods. Perhaps positing a bipedal animal that can exist in the wild is better than having no explanation at all.

When the men of Prince Wales Island are out hunting and hear strange sounds in the woods or see large human-like footprints, they know that there is a Gagiit lurking about. The Gagiit are the lost ones who have returned. Relatives of lost kin are alerted in case it might be their loved one. The Gagiit are described as being very elusive and are usually only seen at a distance. They are reputed to have a varied diet of berries, roots, and deer. They can swim very well and, if you encounter a pile of shellfish shells on a lonely beach, it was probably left by a Gagiit. As usual, they are covered with hair and are very strong. The rumors of them being strong swimmers may account for them being reported on various islands off the coast of North America.

There's another common theme among these creatures that relates to their vocalizations. We often hear sounds like a baby crying or screams and yells attributed to them. One myth that is associated with Prince of Wales Island is that the hairy man or wild men take trees that have been blown down and drive them into the ground upside down to mark their territory. I have seen pictures of this on the Internet that appear to date back to the 1990s because of their resolution and general quality. An investigator went to the island and saw some for himself. They were found in isolated areas and it is very unlikely that someone used heavy machinery to up-end the trees, because there were no machine marks on them. I saw a stand of these up-ended trees in Oregon and got very excited and took some pictures (see Figure 1 on page 3). I haven't found any others since, but I still keep an eye out.

And then there's the Alaska Triangle. This is often compared to the Bermuda Triangle because thousands of people have disappeared there. If you draw a line from Juneau to Anchorage, up to Barrow, and down again, it forms a triangle. It is estimated that four out of every 1,000 people who visit this area have disappeared there. I am sure this is due only to the vastness of the area and the rugged terrain, as well as the fact that there are bears and other large animals that scavenge any remains left behind, but native people in the region have associated the disappearances with some form of mysticism. There are stories of a supernatural shape-shifting being called Kushtata, said to be another form of the otterman, who steals souls from the unsuspecting and transforms some of them into large hairy beasts. In this legend, they seem to be killing two birds with one stone, trying to explain the disappearances of people and the existence of the wild men in one story. When you are captured by the Triangle, you become a man-beast. Two mysteries explained.

THE REALITY BEHIND THE MYTH

A common thread linking the myths and folklore of native people regarding Sasquatches or wild men and women of the woods seems to be offering reasons for why they are what they are. The general idea given by all these myths and legends is that they describe a real creature. Moreover, the narratives are surprisingly similar. Virtually every culture in the Pacific Northwest has some kind of story that tells of a hair-covered wild man. The different names and attributes given to this creature may simply show different perceptions of the beast. For instance, the differences in size may be accounted for by the differences between male and female or adult and juvenile specimens.

While many anthropologists argue that these cultures made up these stories and that they seem to be similar because of cultural interactions, many others believe they are based in reality. The fact remains that there continue to be reports of these creatures being seen, and they are still leaving tracks and other evidence. Moreover, the descriptions given of them remain consistent from folklore to modern encounters. There seems to be a discrepancy in native lore as to whether these creatures are supernatural or simply wild men of the forest, but the baseline mythology seems to reflect the same creature. It all boils down to how detailed the explanation given by the myth or story was intended to be. We see this with the problem of mass disappearances. The otterman or hairy man, when transformed into something supernatural, must still fit within a reasonable explanation. The presence of similar myths and legends outside of the Pacific Northwest re-enforces the notion that this is a real animal.

I visited a petroglyph in southeastern Ohio called the Leo petroglyph, which is attributed to the Fort Ancient culture and is estimated to be around 700 years old. There, among the fish and other carvings, is a perfect carving of a Sasquatch footprint.

Figure 16. Bigfoot footprint in a petroglyph from southeastern Ohio that was carved more than 700 years ago by the Fort Ancient culture, according to the Ohio Historical Society.

It is not shaped like a normal human footprint, but instead is wide, just like the plaster casts of Sasquatch footprints taken in the western United States. I believe this rock carving was used to communicate to traveling tribes what types of fish or game were in the area and to advise them to watch out for hairy men.

The consistency of stories that describe the creature as whistling, either as a form of communication or an instinctive reaction, and the fact that they are always hairy also points to this creature being real. If the native legends were describing other tribes or enemies, I don't think they would say they were covered with hair. Long hair was not uncommon among members of native tribes and it seems unlikely that it would have been considered significant enough to mention as part of the myth. If we encountered a lost or reclusive person in the wild today, they probably would not be covered with hair, although they might need a shave and a haircut. They might be somewhat unkempt, but not furry like an animal.

When we look at the various masks and totems carved by Native Americans, the ones said to depict Sasquatch-type beings are commonly shown to be ape-like in appearance. They show protruding brow ridges, large lips, and sometimes sunken eyes. A majority of myths tell of the creatures stealing food. Several stories have them stealing children, but this is probably used to keep children in line and prevent them from wandering off. A lot of stories contain references to knocking or hitting tree trunks with branches. This is still reported today, and tree-knocking is a tactic used by some investigators to get a response. Is it a coincidence that modern humans report seeing a creature much like that portrayed in native folklore? I think not. If we had the same limited information and knowledge that early natives had, our stories would probably be the same.

8

The Minnesota Iceman and Other Weird Tales

One of the most bizarre and interesting tales in the Bigfoot world concerns the Minnesota Iceman. The origin of the Iceman remains a mystery. He is purported to be a man-like creature that was encased in a block of ice and carried around in a refrigerated truck. Frank Hansen, the keeper of the oddity, said it was entrusted to him by a millionaire from California. He showed it for a fee at fairs and carnivals. One story told that the corpse was found floating in a block of sea ice by a Russian ship in the Bering Sea. The ship docked at a Chinese port and the carcass was seized by authorities and ultimately ended up in Hong Kong. Another story claims the cadaver was found off the coast of Japan, ultimately ending up somewhere in Hong Kong. Yet another tale has the beast coming from Siberia. There are even stories of the creature being shot in Minnesota. Some claimed a woman shot it.

The creature in the ice block was described as a male human-like animal measuring six feet tall, with very large hands and feet. It was covered with dark brown hair that was three to four inches long. One of its eyes was missing, possibly the result of a bullet fired from one of the reputed hunters. One of the arms looked as if it were broken, although no one claimed responsibility for that. It had a large flat nose and thin lips, and was billed as being the "missing link" between apes and humans because of its human form and ape-like traits.

In the late 1960s, Mr. Hansen toured fairs and shopping malls across the country displaying this massive anomaly. Public interest in the creature led to examination by a couple of scientists, one of whom was a cryptozoologist. Ivan T. Sanderson and Bernard Heuvelmans made arrangements to examine this creature to see if it was, in fact, a missing link, or just a sideshow freak. They examined it as best they could without thawing it out. After careful analysis, they determined that the artifact was indeed genuine. Not only that, they concluded that this could actually be a relic Neanderthal. They came to this conclusion because they discovered thawed areas on the corpse where they could see decomposing flesh. This prompted Hansen to commission a replica Iceman to be made in case anything happened to the "authentic" one.

The conclusion that this was a real body caught the attention of law enforcement, who were concerned that, if this were a human being, a crime might have been committed. So Hansen did a switcheroo and showed authorities the fake body. There was even an incident with customs agents, who thought the body might be real.

Sanderson went on to write a detailed article for *Argosy* magazine claiming the authenticity of this historic find. His impressions and first-hand observations, although made through glass and thick ice, were that the specimen had a great bulk and impressive hands that seemed out of proportion, even with its large arms. His overall conclusion was that the Iceman was the corpse of a form of human, humanoid, or hominid, even though it had ponsid, or ape-like, features. The face, or what could be seen of it, appeared to be light in color, a white or pinkish hue. There were no brow ridges and the forehead sloped slightly backward. The molars were prominent and the chin seemed rather wide. One distinguishing feature was the skin folds and wrinkles around the mouth. The eye sockets were large and round, the injury to one eye having caused a considerable amount blood to flow into the ice.

The creature's nose was described as puggish, somewhat like a dog's. Its nasal structure was compared to that of a young gorilla. The torso was very bulky, having wide shoulders and a barrel chest. The arms seemed massive, but were actually rather slender under what appeared to be the longest hair on the body. Only one arm could be seen and this showed a definite break, which may have added more blood to the ice mixture. The upper arm appeared more slender than the forearm and the wrist was very wide. The hands were the most outstanding feature, being quite large, with thick hair on the back. The nails were rather neat, as if they had been manicured. They were flat and yellow in color. The thumbs appeared to be in opposition like a human's.

One intriguing feature of the hand was a large pad located below the thumb that might have served as a cushion if the animal walked on all fours or perhaps climbed trees by grasping branches. The legs were hard to see, since they were encased in the ice, but seemed to be slender and bipedal. The feet were, without a doubt, hominid, but were unusually wide, with short pudgy toes that appeared to be of equal length. There were two thick pads on the feet that could have allowed for traction and maneuverability on snow or loose gravel. They looked as if they were adapted for mountainous terrain.

The article caught the attention of the Smithsonian Institution, which eventually withdrew interest, feeling that the whole creation was a hoax. Hanson stated that he had stored the original body in a freezer as he continued to exhibit the copy into the 1970s. He has since passed away and the whereabouts of the cadaver are unknown. The copy creature was sold on eBay, supposedly for $20,000, and is said to reside somewhere in Texas. Was this really a Neanderthal, or a missing link, or even a Sasquatch body frozen in the ice for all of those years? I don't believe anyone will ever truly know, which only deepens the mystery.

THE MOUNTAIN DEVILS OF APE CANYON

Another strange event, reported by Fred Beck, occurred in July 1924. A group of miners was attacked in what is now Ape Canyon, near Mount Saint Helens, by what some call "mountain devils," large, hairy ape-like creatures known today as Sasquatch, or Bigfoot. Mr. Beck was a colorful character who believed he was clairvoyant and that he had possessed the ability since he was a young man. He had a spirit guide, a woman, who influenced him through the years. Once, when he was in church and fell asleep in the pew, he sensed he had his head in a woman's lap, but there was no one there. As he grew older, he held spiritual meetings and claimed to have visions. After the incident in 1924, he spent years doing healing work.

Beck declared that the spirit of an Indian showed him the location of a mysterious goldmine that would make him rich. He was told that if he followed a white arrow, it would lead him to the entrance to the mine. He and his companions climbed the harsh terrain until one of the group complained that it was a wild goose chase. His spirit guide then told Fred that, since the Great Spirit had been offended, they would never get gold from the mine. Although they found the mine, they never did find a rich vein. They worked the mine for two years, taking samples here and there, and found just enough to keep them digging, but not enough to make them rich.

During this time, they occassionally saw large tracks, but this didn't happen often enough to cause concern, since whatever was making the tracks was leaving them alone. Once, they heard strange sounds that they thought were made by one of them, but weren't. Fred had the impression that the tracks and noises were made by something without physical form, since they had not seen anything. One occurrence that helped convince them that they were in the midst of spirit beings happened by the creek behind their tent, where there was a large sandbar. One of the miners came and got Fred and showed him two large tracks about four inches deep right in the middle of the sandbar. There were no tracks leading to it or coming from it, just the two tracks by themselves. Fred told his companions that whatever had made the tracks had to have dropped down from the sky and then gone back up.

This kind of struck home with me, because, when I was at Salt Fork State Park in Ohio looking for evidence, I had found one track in a meadow with nothing leading up to it and nothing leading away from it. The track was deep, with pronounced toes, so I made a cast. This is not the only track I have found that stood by itself. Kind of makes me think.

In July, the miners had been hearing strange noises in the evening for about a week. They heard whistling noises and what sounded like something beating on its chest. The group was feeling apprehensive but needed to go to the spring to get water. Frank and Hank went, taking their guns just in case. All of a sudden, Hank yelled and raised his rifle. There was a hairy beast about 100 yards away looking from behind a tree. Hank shot and Frank swore that he saw bark fly from the tree. They lost track of the creature momentarily, and then saw it running about 200 yards away, heading into the canyon. Frank shot three more times and it disappeared from sight. They hightailed it back to the cabin and told the others what had happened. Everyone agreed that they would leave in the morning, not wanting to get caught traveling in the dark by these things.

The cabin was hand-built and very sturdy. It had no windows and they had built a fireplace at one end for heat and cooking. It had one long two-man bed and the others slept on the floor, cushioned by soft pine branches. The miners soon fell asleep, but were awakened about midnight by a loud thud against the wall. The wall was hit hard enough to knock chinking from between the logs. They could hear large feet stomping and thrashing about. Then rocks came flying, some hitting the roof and some falling through the chimney into the fireplace. They looked through the space between the logs created by the dislodged chinking and could see three hairy beasts, but assumed there were many more.

They stuck their guns between the logs and started shooting. They shot when they were attacked and backed off when the beasts retreated, trying to demonstrate that they were just defending themselves. They heard the creatures on the roof and shot through the shingles. One of them reached its hand through the logs and grabbed an ax. Fred reached over and turned the head of the axe so it couldn't be pulled through the wall. The beast let the ax go and Fred pulled it back into the cabin. At one point, it seemed that the beasts were trying to push the cabin over, but it was too sound.

The attack lasted most of the night. They came in waves and then backed off. With each wave, the men fired. When the sun came up, the men cautiously went outside. They could see one of the creatures about eighty yards away. Fred lifted his gun and shot. He thought he hit it and it tumbled over a cliff. The men made a hasty exit, leaving behind anything they couldn't carry. They all agreed to keep this to themselves, but the story got out.

Fred returned to the scene with a couple of reporters and a police detective. There were large tracks everywhere, but no sign of the "mountain devils" and no indication that any of them had been shot. Later that year, a great ape hunt was staged, but nothing was ever found. A big game hunter from England showed an interest in pursuing the creatures, and what was referred to only as "a wealthy person" offered a reward for anyone producing a live specimen. People are still reporting that they have seen these creatures in Canada, Washington, northern California, and Oregon, and large tracks are still being found.

The story was told by Fred Beck to his son, Ronald A. Beck, who wrote an account of it in 1967. Since then, there have been no large-scale attacks by these creatures. Fred stated that he believes they were attacked by the beasts because they shot at them. If they had left them alone, he is sure they would have been left in peace. In the years since, there have been many sightings, many tracks found and cast, and many pictures taken. Then the Patterson-Gimlin film was made (see chapter 10) and, through all of this, we still don't have any concrete, tangible evidence of the event. In 1967, referring to the spiritual or supernatural qualities he thought these creatures had, Frank made this statement: "No one will ever capture one, and no one will ever kill one. In other words, present to the world a living one in a cage, or find a dead body of one to be examined by science. I know there are stories that some have been captured, but got away. So will they always get away." So far, this has remained eerily true.

THE BEAST OF MICA MOUNTAIN

In October, 1955, a gentleman named William Roe was working with a road crew near Tete Cache, British Columbia. An avid outdoorsman who was familiar with the area, Roe decided to do some scouting one day, looking for places to hunt. He had shot a bear the year before, so he knew there was game in the area. He climbed a rugged trail on Mica Mountain to where he knew there was an abandoned mine. He had his gun with him, but had no plans to shoot anything. When he reached the mine, which was in an isolated area, he experienced an encounter that is best described by an affidavit that was drawn up on August 26, 1957, by the legal department of the city of Edmonton, Alberta. The affidavit had been requested so the story would be recounted under oath. Here is some of what it contained.

Growing up in Michigan, Roe studied the activities of wild animals and supported his family in Alberta by hunting and fishing. He always admired and respected nature. His most profound experience with a creature occurred around 3 o'clock in the afternoon near a deserted mine. He had left the trail and entered a clearing when he thought he saw a grizzly bear. He was glad he had decided to bring his gun, just in case. He sat on a rock to watch the animal, which was about seventy-five yards away. He could see its head and some of its shoulder.

A few seconds later, the creature got up and stepped into the clearing, walking right toward him. At first, Roe thought it might be a huge man, quite tall and very wide. It had dark brown hair with silver-looking tips all over its body. As the beast got closer, he saw that it had breasts, but not the body of a normal female. It had a thick body with no hips, a straight up-and-down torso. The arms were more muscular than a man's and longer. It had large flat feet and stepped heel-first. The creature got about twenty feet from him and squatted down. It grabbed a brush branch and stripped off the leaves with its teeth. He could see it quite clearly. Its head sat directly on its shoulders and it had no neck. Its nose was wide and flat and its mouth and chin stuck out past its nose. Hair covered its face, except for the mouth and nose. Its ears looked like human ears and its eyes were small and black.

Roe sat there and wondered if this could be someone in a monkey suit, perhaps on location making a movie or something, but no one else was around. After a few minutes, the creature appeared to catch his scent, because it looked right at him with a startled look. He sat still as the creature backed up a few steps, still squatting. It then stood up and walked away. It looked back at him, over its shoulder, not knowing what to make of him. Roe thought for a moment that, if he shot this thing, it could be a great prize to show science and the world. He raised his rifle and looked at the creature. Then he realized that, if the beast were human, he would never forgive himself, so he lowered the gun and watched it walk away. As the creature reached the edge of the clearing, it leaned its head back and made a sound that was half laugh and half language. It then stepped into the brush and disappeared. Roe walked around and found what looked like a spot where it had been sleeping. There was no sign of fire or any tools anywhere. He could not say for certain if the creature was a Sasquatch. Roe then declared that the affidavit was true to the best of his recollection.

Of course, some believed the account and others didn't. The most interesting element of his description was his observation that the creature's breasts were covered with hair. Most primates don't have hair on their breasts. Some made the point years later that Roe's description was recorded seven years before Roger

Patterson's film (see chapter 10). Many believe that Patterson copied the details of Roe's account to fit his own. Both creatures were female with hair on their breasts, both had massive bodies, both showed virtually no neck, both walked away instead of running, and both looked back over their shoulders. The similarities are astounding.

Well, the fact may be that they looked the same because they were the same. If both were female Sasquatch, there is no reason why they should *not* look alike. Female animals of other species look the same. This is no different. Both of these creatures also resemble what is being seen today, although not necessarily female. Patterson was simply at the right place at the right time because he did his homework and knew it was the place to be.

THE WENATCHEE RIVER BIGFOOT

In January 2013 in Wenatchee, Washington, a caller phoned a radio station to report an incident. He claimed to have seen a creature that was about six and a half feet tall and was covered with dark hair. The report also said that the beast was running very fast. An experienced investigator who was listening to the program decided to look into the event, since it had happened locally, near where the Wenatchee River empties into the Columbia River in the foothills of the Cascade Mountains. This area is heavily forested and has a history of Sasquatch sightings that go back many years. The local Native American tribe knows the Bigfoot as Choanito, or night people.

The investigator arrived at the location and looked around in an effort to determine the most likely place to begin. He found a cemetery and an irrigation canal, neither of which were typical Sasquatch habitat. Nearby, he noticed fruit orchards and the remnants of old homesteads. On one side of the road was an orchard that looked well maintained, with younger trees that had been pruned for the coming growing season. On the other side of the road was an older, unkept stand of pear trees. The fruit had not been harvested and there was rotting fruit lying about. With a light coating of snow on the ground, he could see where various fauna had been feasting on the fermenting fruit.

As he walked through the abandoned orchard, he noticed large barefoot prints that looked to be quite fresh. In one far corner of the orchard, he could see a gathering of deer numbering a dozen or so. There were deer tracks in the stand and he could see where they had been bedding. The large tracks in front of him looked as if they could be human, but were much larger. He could not imagine someone walking out there in the snow barefoot, however. The direction of the tracks was toward the tree line at the edge of the orchard. He could tell the tracks were fresh because the snow outline was crisp and sharp, unlike older tracks from deer and fox that had rounded and melting edges. The heel sections of the big tracks were deep and the toe areas were quite wide. In some of the tracks, five toes were prominent.

The investigator contacted a friend to help him document the track line. (It's always good to have a witness to corroborate what you find.) They took measurements and found that the tracks averaged a little over thirteen inches long and were half a foot wide. They determined the stride to be around sixty-five inches. They followed the tracks to a tree that it looked as if the creature had circled several times, perhaps looking for hanging fruit. They then followed the tracks to the tree line, which was close enough to the road for the animal to hide but still see the road. This is where they lost the tracks. The creature could have followed the road through the trees or turned and headed for the foothills. Either way, it left no trace. After tracking the creature as far as they could, they drove to a nearby home-improvement store to get casting materials.

To cast prints in these conditions, you have to stabilize the track using something like spray paint, spray adhesive, or even hairspray. Once you get the track stable, you pour in a fast-drying compound like plaster patch. Luckily, one of the investigators had experience casting prints in the snow and knew the right materials to get. After they had cast several tracks, they began contacting neighbors to see if they could add anything to the investigation. One older lady told them she had seen lots of deer in the orchard, but nothing like a Bigfoot. Another neighbor reported hearing loud crunching noises from the orchard, as if something big were walking through the snow. He had heard deer and bear passing through before, but this was larger. Yet another reported hearing screams or strange shrieking noises a few nights before the sighting. This person raised chickens and added that the flock had seemed really agitated while the shrieking sounds were heard.

The investigator and the neighbor walked up the hill to a stand of pines from which the screams had seemed to come. The pines stood by another irrigation canal that ran above the orchard. They were walking along the bank when they noticed more tracks that were the same size as the tracks the investigator had cast earlier. They looked to be a few days older than the tracks in the orchard, but were still in good condition. They measured the stride and it closely matched that of the other track line.

They also noticed a series of smaller tracks that ran alongside the larger ones. They followed the tracks along a road by the irrigation canal where whatever had left them jumped a fence and climbed a retaining wall, where it left a hand print. This is some of the best evidence the investigator had ever recovered during an investigation. He was amazed at his luck that the sighting had occurred so close to his home so he could get to the site while evidence was still so fresh. He found a map of the area on Google Earth to determine travel patterns the creature might have taken. Then he went on the same radio program he was listening to when he learned about the encounter and talked about what he had found. This encouraged others to contact him and relate their own experiences in the same general area.

One newspaper reported the event, which also generated some interest. There was a misquote in the article, however, which stated that bear footprints had been found in the snow. What it actually should have read was that *barefoot* prints had been found. The overall content of the article was accurate, however, so the basic idea was understood. This is one of the best-documented sightings ever reported because of the investigator's ability to get to the site quickly, before tracks or evidence were lost or contaminated. In most cases, tracks in snow quickly degrade so as to be almost unusable. Another example of being in the right place at the right time.

THE SALMON RIVER DEVIL

Teddy Roosevelt, in his 1893 book *The Wilderness Hunter,* tells of a supposed encounter with a Sasquatch-type creature in Idaho.

An old pelt trapper named Bauman, who had spent most of his days in the high country hunting and trapping, claimed to have a tale to tell. Now these hardy mountain men who lived in God's country weren't usually much taken by tales of ghosts and goblins or hoodoos lurking in the dark. But Bauman said he knew this one was true because he had lived to tell it. And you could tell that he believed it by the fire he showed in his eyes. Bauman had grown up hearing stories of goblins and what not, and legends the Indians told about spirits and apparitions haunting forests, preying on poor souls wandering in the dark. He really didn't put much stock in all that talk, however, until his partner met his fate at the hand of some unknown devil.

Bauman and his partner were setting traps up in the mountains near a fork of the Salmon River. Pelts were few and far between, so they decided to head into a rugged pass where beavers were damming a small stream. The pass was said to be cursed because a hunter had been found there by two miners not long ago, killed by a wild beast. His body had been half eaten. They didn't pay much attention to this, since they both had guns. They followed the trail as far as they could and tied off their horses in a clearing before climbing the rocky path by the stream toward the beaver dams. They found a flat spot to make camp. There was plenty of sign, so they knew they were in the right place. They built a lean-to and unpacked their gear, then headed upstream to scout a bit.

When they returned to the camp, wanting to get there before the sun went down, they found that something had rooted through their belongings, scattering everything about. Curiously, for some reason, perhaps sheer spite, the vandal had knocked down their lean-to. There were tracks around, but they didn't pay them much heed, because they were too busy gathering up their gear and rebuilding their lean-to. Bauman built a fire and started some supper, while his partner examined the tracks. He followed them until they reached a game trail, then came back to the fire and examined the tracks there more closely. After puzzling over them for some time, he said, "Bauman, that bear has been walking on two legs." Bauman thought he was crazy and told him the tracks simply weren't human, but he persisted. Bauman finally looked at the tracks and, after much discussion, they decided they didn't know what they were.

Later that night, Bauman was awakened by some noise and was immediately struck by an awful wild-animal stink. He squinted and saw the outline of something big in the dark. He grabbed his rifle and shot toward the shadow, but he must have missed, because he could hear whatever it was thrashing through the brush. The men stoked up the fire and slept as best they could.

The next morning, they got up and headed to the stream to set beaver traps. They were out the better part of the day then headed back to camp for some grub and tobacco. As they entered camp, they found their gear scattered about again and, again, the lean-to was torn down. They looked around and saw the same tracks they had seen before. And once again, it appeared that the beast walked on two legs. The men rounded up a huge pile of wood and built a fire that would last the night. They decided to take turns guarding the camp. They could hear the creature, or creatures, mulling around in the pines nearby, always keeping its distance and not coming near the fire. They decided that, after daylight, they would gather their traps, pack up, and leave.

In the morning, the pair moved along the stream and found that every trap was empty. They each had a feeling that something was watching them and, on occasion, they heard a branch breaking or a rustling in the brush. By midday, as they neared the camp, they decided to split up since they were both armed and it was broad daylight. His partner went to camp to pack up, while Bauman went to retrieve the last of the traps. He did find beaver in the last couple of traps and took time to skin them. When he was done, he headed for the camp, wanting to head down the mountain to be far from these devils. By the time he got back to the camp, the sun was starting to set. As he neared the camp, he decided he'd better alert his partner so as not to be taken as a devil. He shouted out and waited a spell, but got no answer. He shouted again and still didn't hear anything.

A feeling of dread came over him, because he thought his partner might have left him there. He crept carefully into camp and saw their bed rolls lying there neatly. Then he turned and saw his partner lying on the ground, his rifle at his side. He could tell that his neck had been broken and that he hadn't been dead long. He could see the same tracks all around the body, so he knew what had happened. Bauman ran down the mountain as fast as he could, taking only his rifle. He made it to where the horses were tied and rode all night, not wanting to stop in case the devils were near. Over the years, he told the story many times and swore it was true, so help him God.

Because this story appeared in a book by the twenty-sixth president of the United States, one would think it factual. The idea that a Sasquatch-like creature was written about in 1893 shows that these creature sightings are not a modern phenomenon or something made up or hoaxed more recently. It is terrible to think that a human being was attacked and killed by a Bigfoot. But, as in the 1924 ape-attack story, the creature was shot at, so it makes sense that it would retaliate. Could just be a case of self-defense.

THE OLD MAN OF THE CRATER

When it comes to strange happenings, nothing compares to Major Edward Sturgis Ingraham's account of venturing into a steam cave at Mount Rainier around 1895. Ingraham was a learned man with impeccable credentials. He was the first superintendent of Seattle Public Schools, a member of the State Board of Education, and Regent of the State Agriculture College and School of Science. He was also the founder of the Washington Alpine Club. Ingraham had visited Mount Rainier before and was familiar with the area. He and an associate returned to examine the steam caves related to a crater. Ingraham and his friend descended into the cave and saw unusual marks or scratches on the cave floor. The scratches looked as if two creatures had been engaged in intense warfare. Intrigued by what he saw, he looked for more marks and scratches and found what he thought could be footprints from a large creature. As he and his friend continued deeper into the cave, they found more and more prints.

Then Ingraham started to notice a tingling feeling, like a static charge from a wool rug. He and his friend decided to return to camp, since it was getting late in the day. His curiosity got the better of him, however, and he returned to the cave by himself that evening. He was overcome with excitement as he made his descent. He could feel the warmth of the cave, which added to his anticipation. As he proceeded deeper into the crevasse, he noticed a faint light that drew him in like a moth to a flame. It was as if he were entranced by some unknown force that was guiding him to somewhere he knew he should be. He came upon a fork in the passage and was startled by what sounded like rocks or stones being thrown down it. He stopped and pressed against the wall, waiting for what would come next.

Suddenly, there was the sound of movement and a strange and fearsome creature presented itself. It was a large humanish animal covered with dark matted hair. It had a big head topped with a pointed crown with unkempt hair all about. Its hands and feet were covered with thick dark skin and it had long shiny nails. He knew this wasn't a man, but rather a man-beast separated from humanity eons ago. He was surprised by what it did next. It started rubbing its hands together, creating a strange glow that spread over its entire body. It then started rubbing its large feet quickly against the cave floor, which added to the glow enveloping its body. Without thinking, Ingraham started rubbing his hands and shuffling his feet along with the creature. The beast then raised its fingers, which sparked with pulsating flashes of light.

Ingraham was beside himself. He stood there rubbing and dancing along with this awesome being, as lights flashed and an ember glow engulfed them. A bright light encompassed the creature's crown and an unearthly glow began to join the two figures. They were connecting! The man and the alien creature were somehow connected in thought. The apparition relayed impressions of a race existing within the earth and told of terrible events that had plagued the earth, wiping out its own kind and enabling a new race to emerge. Ingraham gathered his will and shook off the psychic connection, not wanting to follow the creature into the uncertainty of the abyss. He made haste back to the campsite, where he tried to collect his thoughts and consider what his encounter with the old man of the crater might mean.

MUCHALAT HARRY

On rare occassions, some have fallen victim to the Sasquatch. This tale is about a Nootka Indian named Harry who lived on the coast of Vancouver Island and made his living trapping and whale hunting in the Pacific Northwest. One day in 1928, he decided to venture into the deep woods to trap for a couple of months, at least until the weather turned bad. The island was still wild and had plenty of game. He gathered up supplies and made his way to the Conuma River in his canoe, walking the last twelve miles of the rough river before he made camp. He spent some time enjoying the outdoors, feeling at one with nature and all of its glory. It was a beautiful secluded spot and he felt no worries.

Harry was asleep one night by the campfire, rolled up nice and cozy in his bed roll, when he felt as if he were being picked up and tossed about. He was stunned and had no idea what was going on. He opened his eyes and realized he was being carried off by some huge creature. He kicked and screamed, but to no avail, although he was a strong outdoorsman. He knew he had fallen prey to a Sasquatch. He rode on the beast's shoulder for two or three miles, until the creature finally put him down. He could see he was in its camp and that there were about twenty of the beasts gathered around him. Well, Harry had the bejesus scared out of him.

The beasts gathered around him and began pulling on the wool undershirt he had on. Harry looked around and saw bones lying about, some older than others. This must be where they live, he concluded. He figured his bones would be the next ones on the ground. His captors poked and prodded him for awhile and then lost interest and began moseying about. When he saw his chance, he ran like the dickens back to his camp. He jumped into his canoe, braving the current and leaving all his gear except his rifle, and paddled like the wind. He kept it up for a full forty-five miles, until he was found by a missionary priest who took him up to the village for dry clothes and a hot meal. He refused to talk about the ordeal, but bits and pieces of the story came out. The strange thing about old Harry was that, after a few weeks, his hair turned snow white. Harry never did go back and get his gear, and he never ventured back into those woods. More likely than not, the Sasquatch are still there.

9

The World of Bigfoot Researchers

There are only a handful of mainstream scientists investigating the Bigfoot phenomenon. The bulk of these investigation are done by groups, or by individuals combing the woods on weekends or whenever they get the chance. A vast majority of tracks found and cast are discovered by amateurs foraging the countryside. Any new stick structures, hair samples, scat, and other evidence will be found by these front-line troops of the Bigfoot brigade—Squatchers, bobos, and biologists, oh my! Those of us who volunteer our time and efforts to validate this creature and ultimately ensure its protection work tirelessly to achieve this goal. The countless hours we have spent in the woods have brought results, but there is so much more out there to find. When we tell people that we hunt for Sasquatch, they look at us rather strangely. But we just smile, because we know we have a noble purpose. The reasons and methods we use vary from person to person. I look for stick structures and other evidence, because I believe a lot can be learned from this. Others look for tracks and that type of sign, while some investigate sightings to try to establish patterns or frequented areas in which to narrow the search, hoping for an encounter with this elusive and mysterious animal.

The groups I present here all contain dedicated individuals working without pay to identify Bigfoot and other cryptids encountered in North America. They are all driven by a "no kill" philosophy. Unfortunately, there are others who are willing to kill a Sasquatch just to prove that the creature exists. I believe strongly that there are other ways to do this besides dragging in a body. DNA from hair samples or scat or other biological evidence can serve the same purpose. When I investigate, I carry my .45, but only to give my family peace of mind. I would never intentionally shoot or try to harm a Sasquatch in any way, except in self-defense, or in a life-or-death situation. It seems clear that Bigfoot attacks on humans are very rare, more than likely caused by surprising a Bigfoot with its young or by someone acting in a threatening way. There is every indication that this is a gentle and passive animal, and to hunt it for any reason would be criminal.

THE BIGFOOT RESEARCH ORGANIZATION

Probably the best-known group in the Bigfoot field is the Bigfoot Research Organization, or the BFRO. These are the *Finding Bigfoot* guys we have watched on Animal Planet. This team investigates eyewitness accounts from all over the country. In almost every episode, they hold a town hall meeting in which people from the area are invited to relate any experiences they have had. They mark the accounts on a map to determine the best locations to investigate. I was fortunate to be invited to one of these meetings in Canton, Ohio. I had a great time interacting with my fellow Squatchers and listening to the stories they had to tell. The *Finding Bigfoot* crew uses varying, and sometimes unorthodox, methods in an attempt to locate or interact with any Bigfoots that may be in an area.

Founded in 1995, the organization is the oldest and largest group engaged in the hunt for Sasquatch. They are a diverse group of investigators, ranging from scientists to truck drivers, each with their own special talents. The goal of the organization is to study reports and encounters and obtain evidence to support the existence of Bigfoot, but to do so in a way that will cause no harm to the animal. They encourage expeditions into what are considered Bigfoot-active areas, looking for evidence and signs to determine whether the beast is real or not. They were the first to create a database to collect information from around the country about sightings and encounters. The sightings on their website have been investigated and have been determined to be credible. The experience and thoroughness of these investigators indicate that the information reported on the website is valid and authentic.

The team's report-classification system is broken down into classes, depending on the type of sightings that have occurred. Class A sightings are clear visual sightings for which there can be no other explanation. A Bigfoot was seen, misidentification has been ruled out, and all other explanations have been considered. Class B reports occur when a possible Sasquatch is observed at a distance or under less than ideal circumstances. Sounds heard directly attributed to Bigfoot are considered to be in this class. Both Class A and Class B reports must be first-hand observations made by the person reporting the event. Class C reports are second- or perhaps even third-hand reports. These are stories relayed by people who have heard them from others, perhaps losing context and validity in the retelling. The BFRO files these reports for reference, but they are seldom used in the database.

When a sighting is investigated, the potential for discrepancies due to misinterpretation are taken into account more than the credibility of the witness. When Roger Patterson made his famous film of the female Bigfoot (see chapter 10), his credibility was questioned more than the authenticity of the movie. Although he was in the right place at the right time, he was called into question because his motives were suspect. The efforts of the BFRO have popularized the search for Bigfoot and have led to substantial finds, like the London tracks, a track line found in Oregon from which numerous casts were made. Without this organization, a lot of us would be on the couch watching TV on weekends, instead of traipsing through the woods in search of tracks, or possibly a glimpse of the big guy himself.

THE SOUTHEASTERN OHIO SOCIETY FOR BIGFOOT INVESTIGATION

I was once on a camping trip with some fellow Squatchers at Salt Fork State Park in eastern Ohio. The mosquitoes were terrible! It was the middle of August and, as usual for this part of the country, it was hot and humid. My wife was with me, and ours was the only camp that had a generator. My wife took a nap in front of the fan, as the generator hummed in the background. That evening, after a dinner of ham sandwiches and Fritos, Mark, the leader of the group, asked if I would like to go into town to attend a Bigfoot group meeting. Of course, I jumped at the chance.

We went into Cambridge and arrived at the library where the meeting was held. The place was packed. I was told that it was like this every time they scheduled a talk. We found seats, but others had to stand. The group sponsoring the event was the Southeastern Ohio Society for Bigfoot Investigation, or SOSBI, a great bunch of folks who get together to relate their stories and share experiences they have had in the woods of southeast Ohio. One woman who was camping with us said that on Thursday, while they were at the campsite, they thought that a Sasquatch had come into camp in the wee hours of the morning. She was getting up to use the bathroom and made a noise that caused a reaction outside her tent. She said it sounded like a branch breaking, perhaps to alert other Bigfoots that a human was awake. It was cool to think there might be Bigfoots near our camp.

Another story came from an older gentleman who was fishing at night in a small boat with his daughter. He told us that, after the sun went down, they could hear what some call samurai chatter. Two unidentified creatures conversed back-and-forth for about half an hour.

The meeting went on for several hours with more stories being told. This organization does sighting investigations across Ohio, and I signed up to investigate in my area if the need arose. It is this type of grassroots organization that is the backbone of independent investigation. Its members spend days off and vacation time searching for answers and investigating in an intelligent and positive way to ensure that the facts are made clear and the best evidence is presented. This is a shining example of how we Americans do things without official sanction or recognition. I was proud to be able to associate with them.

OHIO BIGFOOT ORGANIZATION

The Ohio Bigfoot Organization, another group of volunteer researchers, was founded as an authoritative and reliable place where witnesses could report their Sasquatch encounters and be treated with understanding and respect, without any preconceptions. This organization strives to pursue all evidence that might document the existence of Sasquatch. Its members work to pass on information in a timely manner so that quick and concise investigations can be pursued that may turn up fresh information that can then be processed and used to identify, classify, and protect this elusive beast of the woods.

This organization has been active for the last several years, along with others, in planning and organizing the Ohio Bigfoot Conference at Salt Fork State Park in eastern Ohio. The conference is held at the Lodge, a great venue for this type of event, with its rustic but comfortable design and accommodations. I have attended and have been a vendor there a few times. They always have interesting guest speakers who lecture and give their specialized seminars. They have even had someone selling Bigfoot cookies, which were a hot item.

The organization has given itself the responsibility of reaching out to the community through lectures and presentations given in small town meetings at libraries and visitor centers, often associating themselves with known authorities in the field. At these meetings, new or current information, local sightings, and new evidence are all shared. They also serve as an outlet for communities to report what may or may not be going on in their locale. This open communication hastens the flow of ideas and theories that may lead to better understanding. It also creates an outlet for those who want to tell their stories or report encounters without fear of ridicule.

I have been to some of these informal and informative meetings. In one, a man relayed his encounter and showed a film he had taken that contained convincing evidence. All of this was presented in a relaxed and comfortable atmosphere. We must create opportunities for this type of dialog in order to build a foundation of knowledge if we hope to solve the puzzle that is Bigfoot.

INDIANA BIGFOOT

The Indiana Bigfoot organization investigates sightings in the Hoosier state. On their homepage, they give details of local sightings and findings. They prefer the name Bigfoot to Sasquatch and other names often used to identify these creatures.

There have been hundreds of reports in this state dating back to the early 1930s and before. One picture from an August 1937 newspaper clipping tells the story of a wild monster seen near the town of Bonneville. Back then, before more descriptive names were given, they referred to these beasts as wild men. Areas of common sightings are listed on their website, including Brown, Jennings, Bartholomew, Lawrence, Monroe, Scott, Orange, and Jefferson counties.

Fifty-one of the ninety-two counties in Indiana have reported sightings. And these are just the sightings that have been reported. Many others could have gone unreported. Reported sightings usually occur in the southern part of the state, which is more heavily forested than the farm lands located in the northern part. This area is also home to the Hoosier National Forest. Spring and fall are considered to be the most active times when encounters are most common, but there have also been sightings in the summer and winter months.

Indiana Bigfoot members carry on a lively debate on their website. Some think that Bigfoots probably migrate and that that is why spring and fall are popular times for sightings, since the creatures would be coming from, or going to, certain destinations. They speculate as to the origins and possible existence of these creatures. Are they cousins of man? Are they interdimensional beings? Are they aliens or supernatural entities? No one knows the exact origins of Bigfoots, or even exactly what these creatures are. There are some who don't even believe that they exist. But the thousands of sightings reported all over the world and the many sightings made closer to home lend credence to their existence.

Indiana Bigfoot members encourage those who have seen, heard, or found evidence of Bigfoots to contact them so they can build a better understanding of what these creatures are and their possible origins. By sharing information, witnesses give researchers needed information and, hopefully, bring them a step closer to solving the mystery. If you have encountered, or know anyone who has encountered these creatures in this area, please contact Indiana Bigfoot with any information you may have to help them learn more about what is going on in their state.

THE ALABAMA BIGFOOT SOCIETY

The Alabama Bigfoot Society declares itself a "No Kill" organization on the homepage of its website. The members of this group express their commitment to researching Sasquatch in a no-nonsense manner. They are "dedicated to the research and preservation of this creature and its habitat." They will not kill, attempt to kill, or associate with anyone who wants to harm this animal or desecrate its habitat. The group has a Native American background and associates Sasquatch with the keeper of the forest, or keeper of the mountain. As a result, they will not allow harvesting of this animal to prove its existence, as they consider it to be a spiritual being. They believe that it has been here since the dawn of time. It has always been here, and will be here when we are gone.

Alabama Bigfoot members make a connection between logging and Bigfoot sightings. When energy costs skyrocketed and logging declined because of fuel prices, the occurrences of Bigfoot encounters decreased. As prices eased and logging resumed, sightings increased. I think that logging and its resulting destruction of habitat definitely affects most woodland creatures, Bigfoot included. Hopefully, some areas will be set aside for wilderness use to give these big fellows some room to roam.

The Alabama researchers believe that Bigfoot is more human-like than anything else, like monkeys or apes. They state that "Bigfoot is not a monkey, not a North American ape." They suggest that they may belong to a race that would rather be left alone by humans. A picture on their website shows what they identify as a teepee structure. Although the structure in the picture resembles some that I have seen, I would not call it a teepee. It is more like a nest than anything else. You can get a feeling for the mood of this site in this quote: "Before we get started, let me add that this is my opinion on the creature. I believe it correct, you may differ. Nevertheless, it is my opinion, and we all know what Clint Eastwood says about opinions." Although his opinions may not agree with the opinions of others, all I can say is God bless the South and their Bigfoot hunters!

THE SIERRA TAHOE BIGFOOT RESEARCH ORGANIZATION

The website of this organization is dedicated to gathering information concerning Bigfoot in the Tahoe and Sierra region of California and Nevada. They investigate eyewitness accounts by people who are willing to discuss their experiences, keeping the information confidential for those who request anonymity. Their goal is to better understand the species in order to protect its habitat and its unique way of life.

This group was inspired by the *MonsterQuest* TV series, which showed episodes of encounters in this area. Research showed that there had been numerous sightings there. This led to an obsession concerning anything Bigfoot and a blog dedicated to Sasquatch. What started out as a hobby turned into a family venture, which ultimately led to field research.

This group's website contains amazing scenery photos and pictures of Bigfoot footprints taken in the area. It also posts stories of run-ins with this creature from surrounding areas. One such story comes from an area called Desolation Wilderness. Friends were camping by a lake that was one of their favorite fishing spots. After a day of catching trout in the cold water, they relaxed by the fire and had some dinner. Later that evening, they were startled by a thud made by a baseball-sized rock hitting the ground a mere ten feet from the them. A minute or so later, another rock hit the ground. They called out, but there was no reply. They turned on their flashlights and walked toward the trail to try to catch whoever was throwing rocks.

All of a sudden, a stick came flying at them. They turned off their lights and ducked behind a tree to see if they could find out what was going on. They heard grunting noises and could hear something large moving in the brush. They saw a huge dark shadow moving across the spillway about 100 yards from them. Whatever it was was gone in an instant. It seemed very unlikely that it was the shadow of another person, since the surrounding terrain was rugged and the creature moved very fast without any light to show the way. Bear and mountain lions don't throw rocks and sticks, and the creature's movements were too quick and agile for it to be a person. They concluded that what they had seen was a Bigfoot. Check out this site for more interesting articles.

KENTUCKY BIGFOOT RESEARCH ORGANIZATION

The website for this group gives team-member bios on its "About" page. Quite a variety of professions are represented within this group. The founder is a high school teacher and IT professional. His wife, who is also a member, works as an administrative assistant. She is credited with bringing curiosity, constructive skepticism, and a fearless attitude to the project. One of the lead investigators is a healthcare worker and senior consultant who also has a doctorate in Public Administration from Tennessee State University. Another is an ordained minister and the founder and president of two church organizations. He is an honorary Kentucky Colonel and is trained in storm and tornado spotting. Yet another is a consultant with a major IT company and an avid sport and outdoor enthusiast whose goal is to further Bigfoot conservation efforts. A student at Indiana University Southeast who is an experienced deep-woods camper also investigates with the group. The military is represented by someone who serves full-time in the Kentucky National Guard and runs a farm in his spare time. His training would be an asset to any group. The group also includes a certified personal trainer with a family. She is a Native American who adds her beliefs and heritage to the endeavor. This seems to be a well-rounded group with intelligent and skeptical members who investigate in a serious manner.

This organization also advocates a no-kill philosophy. Their interest in Bigfoot goes back decades, and is constantly being updated with fresh and new ideas. Their goal is to develop a knowledge base that can further our understanding of this elusive creature. The unique attributes they bring to the research add a strong commitment to this field.

Their website offers a section that attempts to answer the most frequently asked questions. Where is the evidence? Where do they come from? Where are the bones or fossils? Why have we not found a body? They present a list of excellent books for reference, geared toward both veteran and novice Squatchers.

CRYPTIC SHADOWS
PARANORMAL RESEARCH

This unique organization is based in Mississippi. Their website claims that they are willing to investigate just about anything paranormal. I can relate to this group because I originally began my investigations looking for ghosts, and actually had my first Sasquatch experience while in Oregon investigating the Shanghai Tunnels in Portland.

Although based in Mississippi, CSPR (or Kas'per) investigates all over the South. The team has experience in, and is willing to investigate, stories or accounts pertaining to ghostly apparitions, EVP's, ghosts or spirits, demons or demonic activity, cryptid or Bigfoot sightings, hauntings, UFOs, alien abduction, crop circles, animal mutilations, Mothman sightings, strange encounters, unexplained mysteries, and paranormal phenomena. Basically, they'll take on anything that cannot be explained by logical reasoning. This team goes about its varied investigations in a serious manner and approaches each incident in a scientific and technological way.

Its members include a forensic parapsychologist and a demonologist who add professionalism and respect along with confidentiality to their many case studies. They believe that personal ethics are of the greatest importance to ensure that they earn the trust of their clients. The investigations are based on details presented in witness accounts of the events. Proper investigation and experience are used in an effort to uncover any natural causes or misidentification in these accounts, and anything that could be explained by other means. Any evidence collected is presented to clients to either prove or disprove their accounts.

Broadening the range of investigation in this way, in my opinion, makes insights and information from one area available for use in other areas. I have used ghost-hunting techniques in looking for Bigfoot evidence. For instance, I have taken dozens of pictures into the woods from all angles as I would in a haunted area, and have actually caught a few things I might have missed if I hadn't done so. Drawing on other fields enhances information, which can lead to greater discoveries. Using ghost-hunting techniques to hunt Bigfoot and Bigfoot-hunting techniques to look for ghosts can only be of benefit to those out in the field. I have never encountered a Sasquatch in a haunted location, but there is a first time for everything.

THE SOUTHERN OREGON BIGFOOT SOCIETY

This group was founded after an encounter with a Sasquatch in the Oregon Caves National Park. It is unique in that it has joined with the British Centre for Bigfoot Research in order to coordinate their efforts to understand this animal. The founder of the group resided in Alaska for a number of years and is familiar with the outdoors and the variety of animals that inhabit that vast wilderness. His goal is to increase awareness of Bigfoot and to let others know that this creature really does exist. One of the cofounders also lived in Alaska and has hunted big game across the Northwest. He has quite a bit of experience looking for Bigfoot and Bigfoot evidence.

This group has organized many investigations to search the forests and mountains of Oregon for signs of Bigfoot. They have discovered footprints as well as hand prints, and have collected hair samples. They have seen large boulders placed in roadways that were too heavy for a man to have moved adjacent to large branches broken off trees ten feet from the ground. They make use of piles of fruit placed in active areas as bait and set trail cameras to watch them. They dampen the ground around the bait to increase the chance of finding tracks. They have seen fruit with large, unidentified teeth marks in it.

The group also uses other techniques, like call-blasting recorded Sasquatch sounds to try to get a response. This has been used successfully many times. Once, on an expedition in southern Oregon, they used bait piles to lure the big guys in. They placed one pile some distance away and another closer in, hoping that would lead the animal to them. They had a camera monitoring the second pile that was linked to a monitor at base camp. The first pile was hit, but not the second. It seems as if the creatures could tell that the other bait was being monitored. There have been many stories about Sasquatch being able to recognize camera traps, and this may be what happened in this case. Just shows how intelligent this creature really is. Investigations continue in the southern part of Oregon, which seems to be the most active area. It is almost as if the more we learn about this creature, the more they learn about us.

EAST TENNESSEE BIGFOOT

Founded in 2005, this group believes that Bigfoot lives and thrives in their fair state. It has long been known that Bigfoot has been reported across the country, especially in areas of the Pacific Northwest, but Tennessee has also had their share of sightings. Detailed reports of these events have been included on many sites on the Internet. Moreover, some believe that many sightings in east Tennessee go unreported. The purpose of this group is to remedy this by investigating and gathering information about reports in their area.

The reports they look into remain confidential and they never require payment. If asked, they will visit the location of a sighting and poke around a bit. The founder was inspired by watching Bigfoot shows back in the 1970s. He found out what he could from books in the library, of which there were few, until the Internet became the main source for information. There is no shortage of Bigfoot lore on the web. He absorbed all of this information, along with the different theories as to what the creature might be and where it may have come from.

In 2005, the founder's son had a Bigfoot encounter right in his own backyard. He could hardly believe that something like that could happen so close to home, until a couple of weeks later a neighbor told him that he had also seen a "gorilla-looking thing." Noises were heard back in the woods that sounded similar to those made by a Bigfoot. The father and neighbor contacted a prominent Bigfoot organization about the encounter, but the sighting was ignored for some reason. Eventually, they founded their own group to investigate the reports. This is how the East Tennessee Bigfoot organization was born, to fill the need felt by residents to investigate local sightings. They handed out business cards to off-road riders and posted broadsides on store bulletin boards encouraging everyone to report any activity they had seen or heard. Needless to say, a few crazy stories turned up, but then actual sightings started to trickle in and they finally got into some real investigative work. The group prides itself on being honest and straightforward. If they ever do find their elusive creature, however, they'll be glad to take the credit.

TRI-STATE BIGFOOT

Closer to my home turf is Tri-State Bigfoot. Founded in 2009, this group has active searches in progress for evidence of Sasquatch and what we in Ohio call the Ohio Grassman. Their goal is to develop patterns of possible migrations and diet through scientific research. They collect evidence and present it for public evaluation to determine its validity. Any evidence collected is compared to popular theory to identify possible hoaxing. All members undergo training in the use of advanced technology and evidence collection, along with safety and animal-identification courses.

As with other credible groups, they do not charge for their services and all information remains confidential. Although the group is based in southwestern Ohio, they include Kentucky and Indiana in their research. Investigators include those trained in operations and web design, and a sketch artist who contacts witnesses and joins in investigations to give a better understanding of the topography of an area as they look for potential food resources. The group also researches moon phases. Some scientists don't believe that Sasquatch has adaptated to be nocturnal, since a vast majority of primates aren't. But some believe that these creatures move or hunt during full moons because they can see better at those times.

The group is committed to presenting any findings in a scientific and logical way, never presenting speculation or unproven theories as fact. They conduct public events on occasion to highlight evidence they have collected or encountered, but they always maintain their commitment to privacy for witnesses who request it. This organization has been on several radio programs and contributed to magazine articles. They have also been mentioned in several books. They only involve themselves with those who portray this phenomenon in a positive way, however. They do not accept gratuities for any work done, but they are willing to participate in charity work if it is for a good cause.

On their website, they have some interesting blogs, one of which discusses various petroglyphs in the tri-state area. This is interesting to me because of the Leo petroglyph that I saw in southeastern Ohio with what looks to me like Sasquatch-type footprint carvings in the rock (see Figure 16 on page 31). This and other carvings go back for centuries. I can appreciate their enthusiasm.

OPERATION DISCOVERY

This group, located in the Pacific Northwest, is made up of private individuals who undertake field investigations and evidence collecting. Their goal is to better understand Sasquatch and to help others with this understanding. They operate on funds generated by the sale of video documentaries. They maintain field excursions in the Northwest, as well as in Alaska and British Columbia, because of increased activity in these areas.

Operation Discovery uses state-of-the-art technology in an effort to document Sasquatch activity in the Cascade Mountains. They set up sophisticated surveillance equipment during winter storms, because it is possible that Bigfoots may be driven by the storms to lower altitudes, probably during low light to avoid being seen. The Cellular Field Surveillance System they have developed now has upgraded audio as well as fragrance attraction abilities. They believe they have the ultimate Sasquatch-detecting system, one that is free of most human contamination and can be monitored from remote locations. This equipment has been tested in adverse conditions and performed well. Their first documentary is part of a two-disk set.

The second documentary is entitled *Sasquatch of Canada.* The area of investigation in this segment is the mountains of British Columbia. Investigators documented a one-week venture into the high mountains, penetrating into isolated locations and having incredible encounters. Several of these creatures were tracked for miles through wilderness and rugged terrain. Using their high-tech equipment, they could catch strange vocalizations at night that indicated the presence of Bigfoot. Investigators were filmed casting Sasquatch footprints so they could be returned to civilization for further study. Researchers documented the team looking for and finding incredible evidence that added to the proof that this creature exists. The information presented in documentaries like these and the pursuit of this creature by this organization adds to the knowledge and mystery that is Sasquatch. The time and effort required to make these programs, to say nothing of the expense, shows the dedication and drive these researchers have to bring their find-ings to the world in a professional and informative way.

THE NORTH AMERICAN WOOD APE CONSERVANCY

This organization consists of volunteer scientists, naturalists, and investigators working together as a nonprofit Sasquatch research organization. Its more than sixty members are dedi-cated to pursuing research and education for a better under-standing of the nature of the wild men, or hairy ones. They believe that an uncategorized large great ape inhabits the for-ests of North America and they are dedicated to proving this theory. This group is funded by dues paid by its members and by conferences, fundraisers, grants, and donations. No member is compensated, and no funds are used for member activities.

NAWAC seeks credibility and acceptance leading to sci-entific classification of this animal. Their goal is official rec-ognition for and protection of this animal and its habitat. Its members include a wildlife biologist, an anthropologist, teach-ers, a wildlife ecologist, a military intelligence officer, and a businessman, among others. They are convinced that there is much to learn about the earth, the oceans, and animal species that remain hidden in forests and jungles, as well as under the waves. They concentrate their efforts on proving the existence of the wood ape, which would be one of the greatest and most controversial discoveries in the history of mankind. Such a dis-covery would create an outcry for conservation and legitimate passive study, since there could be a human heritage associated with this creature.

Their website contains a wealth of information from all aspects of wood-ape investigation. They present evidence that includes footprint casts as well as hair samples. All information is updated regularly. They describe the latest sightings from around the country as well as their own investigations. They feature blogs from different informed individuals and offer insight into what others are doing in the field. The site also contains sections that discuss hoaxes and false evidence that have been presented to experts, who give their professional opinion concerning these matters. There is evidence out there that has been proven false that is still presented as factual. There is also a question-and-answer section that addresses many issues in a concise and logical way based on evidence collected, eyewitness observations, and common-sense scientific principles. This group is well worth checking out for both novices and experienced researchers.

NEW YORK BIGFOOT SOCIETY

This group dedicates itself to finding "beasts of global infamy," and those of myth and folklore. Its members are all well-trained and informed concerning cryptozoology and paranormal topics. Their expertise includes primate and animal behavior, as well as archaeology, anthropology, and psychology. Their use of high-tech equipment rounds out an expertly trained and equipped outfit. Their research area includes all of New York, and they have ventured into Vermont. Their goal is to study the hotspots that occur in their areas of interest. One of their newest team members is a beagle named Jet, who has been trained in both hunting and tracking. The use of a dog in their investigations is unique and may lead to better evidence retrieval. This is a different way of doing things that others should note.

The team endeavors to help witnesses understand their claims and realize what was actually going on in order to dispel their fears. Their ultimate goal is to present verifiable and irrefutable evidence for the existence of cryptids and other species unknown to the world.

10

Investigations and Noteworthy Evidence

When we talk about investigations concerning Bigfoot and Sasquatch, the discussion would not be complete without a discussion of the Patterson-Gimlin film, which was taken in northern California in 1967. To some, this is the Holy Grail of proof that cryptids exist. This film has probably been examined more than the Zapruder film taken at the Kennedy assassination. I have seen documentaries that examine it frame-by-frame to determine whether it is genuine or a hoax. Many say it is authentic and others say it is a man in a gorilla suit. There was even someone who claimed he was the man in the suit.

The creature portrayed in this film has obvious female characteristics, which would be hard to fake using 1967 technology. Moreover, when examined frame by frame, there is a bulge that shows up on the creature's right leg that is explained as a muscle tear that protrudes when it walks, another feature that would be very hard to fabricate. The creature's gait has been examined over and over again, and many have determined that it is not a human gait. The legs are too short for the torso, which is another point that can't be faked. A man in a gorilla suit is just that. His legs are still the same length in proportion to his body. Arms can be lengthened using extensions, but legs really can't be shortened. The way the head turns with the body is another point of interest.

Footprints were found in the creek bed after the creature walked through that were cast and put on display. The fact that the filmmakers just happened to be at the right place at the right time with a camera has been questioned, but it may have been just that—luck. When I hunt deer, I have to be at the right place at the right time with the right equipment in order to get my deer. It takes planning and scouting to make sure I'm in the right place, and I must know that there are deer in the area by reading sign. I believe these men were there because they did their homework and had an idea that they might encounter a Bigfoot because they were in Bigfoot territory. I don't believe they were there just by chance. They were there because the Sasquatch were there. And the rest is history. Here is how the legendary story goes.

THE PATTERSON-GIMLIN FILM

Bob Gimlin, a builder and rancher from Yakima, Washington, had his first experience with Sasquatch in British Columbia when on a trip with his wife. They saw a sign that said they were in Sasquatch country, which they mistook to mean Native American territory. Bob's friend Roger Patterson had read a newspaper article published in 1959 about a strange creature that is supposed to live in the mountains of northern California and he became intrigued with the possibility. In 1964, he went to Willow Creek, where he met some of the locals, saw plaster casts of footprints found in the area, and heard stories about encounters with the beast. Roger showed the footprint casts to Bob, who wasn't really convinced, but was willing to listen. Maybe there was something to this after all.

Bob and Roger went to investigate sightings that had been reported around Yakima and other areas. On horseback, they looked around Mount Saint Helens, which was supposed to be a Bigfoot hotspot. Some friends in Willow Creek told them that there had been recent sightings and that several tracks had been found. Roger was in the process of making a documentary about Sasquatch and thought this would be a great opportunity to find some evidence. So Roger and Bob gathered up their gear, put a couple of pack horses in the trailer, and headed out for Willow Creek. By the time they got there, rain had washed away any tracks that might have been left. They set up camp and started roaming the dirt logging roads looking for tracks. Sometimes they split up to cover more territory. They did this for a couple of weeks, hoping to find any signs of the elusive man-beast.

On October 20, 1967, Bob got up and rode around a bit by himself, not finding much. When he got back to camp and met up with Roger, they decided to ride into an area they had been in not too long before. As they rode along, with Roger in the lead and Bob behind towing a pack horse, they rounded a fallen log with a bunch of debris piled up around it and came upon a creek with a sandbar. All of a sudden, they saw the creature. It was about eighty feet from them and it stared straight at them. The horses were startled by the creature and started panicking. Roger tried to settle his horse while reaching for the camera. He had once been a rodeo rider, which helped him through the situation.

Roger jumped off his horse holding the camera. He splashed through the creek and ran toward the sandbar with the camera up and rolling. He fell to his knees on the sandbar. The creature turned and started walking up the sandbar along the creek. Bob crossed the creek with his horse and pulled the 30.06 he had by the saddle. He jumped down from the horse, ready to shoot if the creature attacked. They had made a pact not to shoot anything they found unless it got violent or attacked them and they had to shoot in self-defense.

The creature looked back at Bob as he crossed the creek and was only about sixty feet away. Roger was busy trying to get into position to get a good camera angle when it looked back again. This is when they captured the famous turn and stare that the creature made. It all happened quickly and was over in a moment. They stood there for a minute asking themselves: "Did this really happen? Did we really just see that?"

The creature was huge, but very graceful. It moved along with hardly any effort despite being massive and heavy. It appeared to be about six and a half feet tall and to weigh at least 500 pounds. It was muscular and bulky. They looked around and found the deep tracks it had left behind, taking pictures of them and making plaster casts. Bob described the face and eyes of the creature. It had a flat nose and lips through which he could see its teeth. Its eyes were large, and the hair on its face seemed short and sparse. It swung its arms like a human. He could see its muscles flexing, which convinced him that it wasn't someone in a monkey suit. After all, who would be foolish enough to do something like that in the middle of the woods, seeing that Bob was armed? The creature looked female, but without ever having seen one, Roger couldn't be sure. The film later showed what looked like mammary glands, so they concluded that it was female.

The tracks they had found previously seemed to indicate that there were three of the creatures in the area, perhaps a male, a female, and a juvenile. It was a bit unnerving to them, knowing that there could be more of these creatures around, especially an adult male. Bob wanted to follow the beast, but their uncertainty as to its nature kept them from going after it. The pair returned to town and told people that they had got the "son of a buck." News soon got out about the film and the tracks they had found. Some thought it was the greatest discovery ever, but some just thought it was trickery. They figured Roger had faked the whole ordeal just to make money and a name for himself. Trouble is, no one could tell which. The story and controversy continue to this day.

FINDING BIGFOOT

The Animal Planet channel airs an entertaining show called *Finding Bigfoot*. The show recounts the adventures of a group that goes to areas where someone has experienced a Bigfoot sighting, either catching it on film, or taking pictures, or recording sounds. They hold town hall meetings to encourage stories from witnesses in the area and map the sightings to determine if there is a pattern to them. Then they do an investigation based on this information. Members include Matt, who got his start in Ohio; Bobo, who has been investigating Bigfoot for years; Cliff, a schoolteacher and Bigfoot investigator; and Ranae, a field biologist and Bigfoot skeptic.

The team does its investigations at night, because they believe Sasquatch is nocturnal, even though there have been numerous daytime sightings. As I have said, I believe the creatures have a segmented sleep pattern that leads to day or night sightings, but I don't have any substantial proof. The fact that a vast majority of primates are not nocturnal and those that are exhibit special adaptations leads me to think they are probably not nocturnal. There is a theory, however, that they move at night in order to hide from humans, because humans are not necessarily active at night.

The Animal Planet team has come up with some very interesting methods to draw in Bigfoots, who they contend are very curious. This may very well be, because they have to learn about us somehow in order to stay one step ahead of us. The team has used methods like setting off fireworks, holding a luau, or having a group of Girl Scouts giggle and make noise. They have set out doughnuts and rotting guts, and once they had a barbecue to entice the creature. I think my favorite attempt was when Cliff played a bass guitar in the woods. I like this because I also play a bass.

The team has investigated all over the country and in several places overseas. They did an investigation in Washington State during which they heard voices that they attributed to possible Bigfoot chatter. I believe, being a ghost hunter, that they were actually hearing the disembodied voices of ghosts. I myself have heard them, so I know for a fact that this does occur. Of course, one of my favorite episodes is the one in which they investigated Salt Fork State Park in eastern Ohio. Since I have been there several times myself, I can relate to the areas they were in.

This group has received some very interesting evidence, including photos, camcorder footage, thermal-imaging pictures, and voice recordings. One of the more compelling videos was actually taken in the 1950s in Colorado. It showed a hairy beast at some distance, crossing a snowy field by walking on boulders, seemingly not wanting to leave any tracks. Another video was shot by students in Idaho. Upon seeing it, Dr. Jeffrey Meldrum stated that it reminded him of the Patterson film discussed earlier. It shows a creature in a wooded area getting up and walking away. Another nice piece of evidence came from Florida, where a couple had been visited by a Sasquatch (or Skunk Ape) who had left a greasy handprint on a porch door. They also appeal to local Native Americans to share their stories of sightings and their experiences.

The Animal Planet team returned to northern California with Bob Gimlin and actually visited the area were the original Patterson film was shot, retracing the steps and recreating circumstances that had led to that fateful encounter. They have also traveled to Australia to look for the Yowie, a Bigfoot-type creature reported to inhabit the outback. During a town meeting they held in Australia, they heard some strange stories, one of which was from a man who said the beast had stolen his goats and placed them along a tall branch after disemboweling them. Strange indeed.

In Sumatra, they searched for the Orang Pendek, a much smaller cousin of the Bigfoot. This cryptid is thought to be a relic population of *Homo Floresiensis*, whose fossil remains were found on the island of Flores in Indonesia. This human relative stood a mere three feet tall and survived until about 13,000 years ago. There is a very good possibility that this creature exists today and is either a relative of, or actually is, a *Homo Floresiensis*. It has been nicknamed the Hobbit in homage to the diminutive characters created by J. R. R. Tolkien in fantasy fiction.

The *Finding Bigfoot* team has also been to Vietnam to look for the Nguoi Rung, or Batutut, which may be a descendent of *Gigantopithecus*, since it isn't very far from where they found the original *Gigantopithecus* fossils. In China, they pursued the Yeren, another possible *Gigantopithecus*. During their excursions, they found only circumstantial evidence, perhaps because they were unfamiliar with the area and terrain. I don't hunt deer in areas I haven't scouted and don't know well. They went to New York State to investigate a video of what seems to be a young Bigfoot climbing around in a tree. It looks as if the smaller creature jumps from the shoulder of a larger one and swings around like an orangutan. They believed it was a juvenile Bigfoot, but, in my opinion, it looks like someone's pet. Since I wasn't there, I can't make a judgment call, but I am skeptical of this one.

This team has done some crazy things trying to draw in a curious Bigfoot, and they have investigated some pretty strange encounters. I'm sure they have the best intentions, but some of what they do seems to serve only to enhance the entertainment value. After all, it is a TV show. They have to make it interesting enough for people to keep watching. Despite this, however, they really do demand our respect. They are out there doing the best they can to investigate this phenomenon. They are trying to bring understanding and credibility to the search for this giant, and they do it in a nondestructive and passive way in order not to damage nature or cause harm to the Sasquatch in any way. That is the way it should be. They are out there doing much-needed work. I offer them my thanks.

THE SKOOKUM CAST

The meager evidence left by Bigfoot includes rare footprints, sometimes a hair or two, perhaps a knuckle or hand print, cryptic stick structures, and one large impression that is believed to be that of the creature itself. This impression is referred to as the Skookum cast. It was found in the Cascade Mountains of southern Washington State near an area called Skookum Meadow by a group of investigators doing an extensive Sasquatch search using call-blasting, thermal imaging, and night-vision photography. They located several sets of tracks that were not immediately identified.

The investigators included Derek Randalls, a professional landscaper, Leroy Fish, a professional wildlife ecologist, and Richard Noll, an aerospace meteorologist. They set up an area where they used pheromone scents and fruit as bait. When they returned to the area, they found that some of the bait was missing. Some of the fruit pieces were scattered about and, among them, there was an unusual impression that seemed to have been made by the body of a large, hairy animal. An impression of the hair had been left in the soft clay. The team examined the impression, trying to determine what could have made it. They approached it scientifically, attempting to eliminate possibilities and variables. They compared the impression to animals that roamed the area, including elk, deer, bear, and even coyotes. None of these possibilities matched the size, shape, or bulk of what had made the impression. The only possibility they couldn't rule out was a Sasquatch.

The outline and impression of the creature show the imprint of a left forearm, buttocks, thigh, and what look like heels. The investigators looked for footprints leading up to the impression, but the ground around the area was too hard for prints. The impression had been left in a drying puddle on the side of a forest-service road. The clay was soft enough to capture an impression without really sticking to anything. The trio examined the scene and formed the hypothesis that the Sasquatch had crept up to get the bait and deliberately left no tracks. This is recognized Sasquatch behavior. They often avoid leaving tracks or other sign for humans to follow.

The posture and position of the impression seem to indicate possible primate physiology, as they tend to remain upright when holding on to tree trunks. It is easy to imagine a Bigfoot resting on its forearm and reaching for the fruit. The print is definitely that of an animal, since there was body hair impressed into the clay. There were tracks in softer areas along the road, some belonging to elk and coyote, but they did not lead in the direction of the the impression. The only animal large enough to make this print might have been an elk. Even though the measurements of the imprint seemed incorrect, the possibility of an elk had to be considered.

The team gathered up all of their plaster to make a cast—about 200 pounds altogether. The casting they made measured three and a half by five feet, and it was carefully loaded onto a cushion in the back of a pickup truck. Once the cast arrived back in town, they made arrangements to clean and examine it. Observations, measurements, and comparisons were made. They measured the length and depth of the impression, which appeared to be of a large hominid. The body dimensions indicate that the creature had a body density that is 40 to 50 percent greater than that of a six-foot-tall man. The heel print, upon examination, exhibited what look like dermal ridges that fingerprint expert Jimmy Chilcutt said were consistent with ridges found in some Bigfoot track casts. The impression also revealed the back of the leg and the Achilles tendon, which is a feature of a bipedal primate.

Over time, researchers made casts of impressions of elk and other animals at game preserves and zoos. These were studied by various professionals and consultants, who, after long consideration, determined that they did not match the Skookum cast. The elk was eliminated because, when an elk gets up from a mud wallow, its hooves are directly underneath it and leave definite hoof prints. There were no such tracks in the Skookum cast. This leaves only one obvious conclusion.

BIGFOOT: THE DEFINITIVE GUIDE

In 2011, a group of scientists were assembled to make a documentary called *Bigfoot: The Definitive Guide*. The panel consisted of Dr. Jeff Meldrum of Idaho State University, a known Bigfoot field researcher; Dr. Anna Nekaris of Oxford Brooks University, UK; Dr. Bill Sellers, an authority on ancient humans; Dr. Jack Rink of McMaster University, Canada; and Ian Redmond, field biologist. This group was assembled to try to establish a consensus on what Bigfoot might be from sightings, physical evidence like hair or tracks, and sounds like cries or vocalizations. They examined the Patterson-Gimlin film in detail. Their opinion as to whether this was a real animal or a hoax was divided. Two members of the team believed it was a real animal; two thought it was a hoax; one was undecided. The skeptics among the group thought the creature looked like a man in a gorilla suit, but this opinion was based on the history and demeanor of Roger Patterson rather than on the evidence itself. They felt that Patterson was dead set on filming a Bigfoot, so he did so by fabrication. I think he caught the Bigfoot on film because he placed himself in the right area to do so. He insisted the film was real until his dying day.

This panel also considered stories from the area of Chilliwack, British Columbia. One story relates the experiences that two women had in July 1934. The women were living in a cabin in a wooded area outside of town. They were alerted to something moving around outside of the cabin by the dog barking. They could see something moving in the trees, but couldn't make it out. As they watched nervously through a window, a giant suddenly appeared just outside. Startled by what they saw, the women screamed and the creature left, not leaving much sign.

On another occasion, in September 1941, Jenny Chapman was hanging laundry on a clothesline by their house, which was located some distance from town. Her children were playing nearby. In the distance by the tree line, she saw something moving. At first, she thought it was a bear, but, as she watched, she knew it was something different. Then the hairy giant started approaching the house. She gathered up her children and took off down the road, all running for their lives. Later that day, her husband returned home to find his family gone and the house ransacked. In the back of the house, he found their 300-pound fish barrel had been smashed and the fish were gone. He later found his family in town. They never returned to the house.

Stories like these circulated around Chilliwack in the 1930s and 1940s, and the area soon became known as a hotspot for Bigfoot activity. Researchers discussed whether or not there was an ample food supply there to support a population of Sasquatch. After examining resources, they determined that there was. On the coast, there are various shellfish in tidal pools. Inland, there are fish and mollusks. And, if properly adapted, the creatures could subsist on various plants and berries. The availability of food was dismissed as a problem, especially in coastal areas where there isn't much snow.

The discussion then turned to what fossil evidence there was for the existence of Bigfoot. The most obvious was the discovery of *Gigantopithecus* teeth and mandibles in China, and the possibility that the Yeti could be a relative of Sasquatch. The possibility that *Gigantopithecus* and variations of the species could have crossed over a land bridge from Asia was a real one. The problem that there aren't any fossil records of this migration, or fossil records of Bigfoot, remains however. The fact that the environment of the Pacific Northwest is really not conducive to fossil formation, plus the fact that the land bridge isn't there any longer, doesn't help the case.

Several theories were presented as to what these creatures could be. One was that they are a relic population of pre-humans that have survived. There are various stories from Russia and northern Asia about encounters with Neanderthal-type creatures. As we have seen, the largest human ancestor was *Homo Heidelbergensis*, who stood between six and seven feet tall. Remains of this giant have been found that date to as recently as 12,000 years ago. In the 1800s, two prospectors reported coming across a beast in northern California that met the description of a pre-human being.

Another theory offered was that Bigfoot sightings are misidentified Native Americans undergoing shamanic training. The shamans lived in the wilderness alone for up to ten years to learn the ways and secrets of nature. The fact was brought up, however, that this would not account for the massive tracks that have been found and cast. If the Patterson-Gimlin film is considered to be that of an actual animal, then the most plausible explanation for this hidden primate is that Sasquatch is a descendent or relative of *Gigantopithecus*. Without DNA or other concrete evidence, this is purely conjecture. This could very well be a unique and different species altogether. The group determined that it is possible for such an animal to exist, since there is ample food and habitable area for this creature to maintain a viable population.

11

Bigfoot in Pop Culture

B igfoot is alive and well . . . and living in Western culture. On August 27, 1958, Jerry Crew introduced Bigfoot to the American public. With his newspaper article, which high-lighted plaster casts, the world awakened to the possibility of monsters stalking us in the forests of North America. This could be compared to Christopher Columbus discovering the New World. For centuries, the Vikings and Norsemen knew of the land west of Greenland, which is now Canada and North America. They had settlements in this region long before Columbus made his discoveries. All Columbus did was open the New World to exploration and exploitation.

There have been reports of a wild man in northern Califor-nia for quite a long time. Native American cultures from Alaska to California and beyond have historically believed in a hairy man of the forest and they have many names for it. They have made pictographs and petroglyphs of this creature that indicate it is a real entity. Sightings of the wild man have been made by settlers ever since Europeans first arrived. These have been reported in various newspapers, along with footprints that have been found.

On September 27, 1870, the *Daily Transcript* ran a report of two gentlemen, F. J. Hildreth and Samuel DeGroot of Washington Corners, California, discovering strange human-like footprints on Orias Timbers Creek while on a hunting trip. The tracks were said to resemble those of a human, but were larger and with broader toes. Sometime later, Mr. Hildreth, having become separated from his fellow hunter, reported seeing something ahead of him that he believed was a gorilla. Apparently, sightings of these gorilla-like creatures had been reported there before.

On January 2, 1886, the *Del Norte California Record* printed an account of Mr. Jack Dover, an upstanding member of the community, who reported an amazing sighting while on a hunting foray. He told of seeing a thing of gigantic size standing about 150 yards away picking berries from a bush. He described it as being about seven feet tall, with the head of a bulldog, short ears, and long hair. Its voice was shrill and very human-like, comparable to that of a woman in great fear. He found no footprints, for the ground was quite hard and dry. He aimed his gun at the creature several times, but was overcome with the feeling that it could be human. Others had seen this beast in the area and most agreed with Dover's description. This animal appeared to be an herbivore and was said to winter in the caves of Marble Mountain.

The footprints that Jerry Crew found were not the first, and they were certainly not the last. Tracks had been found and sightings had been made for a very long time, but his report was the one that caught everyone's attention, the one that created the frenzy. Crew's report brought Bigfoot into the spotlight of Western culture. Today, there are very few people who have never heard of Bigfoot. As with Columbus and the New World, Jerry Crew opened the phenomena of Bigfoot to exploration and exploitation.

BIGFOOT BOOKS

On Amazon, you can find well over 100 book titles devoted to Bigfoot and Sasquatch. These publications range from scientific examination to Bigfoot erotica (yes, it does exist). There is so much written on this subject, yet we know so little about it. Those of us who do write about it examine evidence, found or presented, in an attempt to paint as accurate a picture as we can of the realities of this creature. I have used several of the more informative books to create a foundation of knowledge on which to build during my investigations.

Probably the best book on the subject is *Sasquatch, Legend Meets Science* by Dr. Jeffrey Meldrum. This book deals with legitimate scientific theory and practical facts. Dr. Meldrum has spent a career examining footprint evidence and has determined Bigfoot to be an actual unknown primate. He is considered to be at the top of this field. There are very few, if any, who have more knowledge about the characteristic locomotion of this animal. Dr. Meldrum recognized a mid-tarsal break in print casts that indicates a significant difference between Sasquatch and human foot construction and walking styles. This, and the recognition of dermal ridges, adds to the authenticity of this creature.

If you want to research the history of this beast, I recommend *The Historical Bigfoot* by Chad Arment. I had the opportunity to talk to Chad several years ago at an Ohio Bigfoot Conference at a dinner presided over by John Mionczynski. Arment is a very cool guy, and a fellow Buckeye. His book is the premier reference for historical accounts concerning Sasquatch, arranged state-by-state. It reports accounts that predate the recent cultural phenomenon of Bigfoot in North America, from the early 1800s until the 1940s. This book does not concern itself with Native American mythology, except for a few examples, but concentrates rather on sightings of the wild man, gorillas, "what-is-its," yahoos, and nondescript beasts encountered and reported by those who could not identify what they had seen. Most of the reports are taken from newspaper stories of the day. Arment takes care to omit obvious hoaxes, false stories used to boost circulation, and fraudulent claims. Even though myth and folklore have been eliminated, however, the reports in this book add credence and probability to myths and folklore.

One book that does address Native American folklore and legend is *Raincoast Sasquatch* by J. Robert Alley. This is a collection of first-hand accounts, historical reports, and native folklore from the rain-drenched forests of the Pacific Northwest.

Alley was fascinated by stories and newspaper reports of the beast called Sasquatch in his native Manitoba, and the subject was always in the back of his mind as he pursued a career in physical therapy. On a backpacking vacation in the Rocky Mountains near Nordegg, Alberta, in the summer of 1973, he found a strange track. It measured sixteen inches long and had five toes with no claw prints, indicating that it did not belong to a bear. Being familiar with human anatomy, he knew it was unlikely that the print belonged to a person, even one with some type of pituitary disorder. This set his mind working on the possible existence of Sasquatch. After moving to Vancouver Island, British Columbia, he met with Sasquatch researchers and began compiling information and stories to support the existence of the creature. This book is the result of years of interviewing witnesses, field research, and ethnographic investigation.

When we consider different aspects that make Sasquatch such a profound enigma, one book stands out as testimony that this creature has an actual language and the ability to communicate verbally. The fact that they can talk to and understand one another indicates a high degree of intelligence. The book *Voices in the Wilderness*, written by Ron Morehead, details the experiences of a group of hunters in the Sierra Mountains of California during the early 1970s. During various treks into the wilderness, they encountered vocalizations of what could be a family unit of Bigfoots that had settled near their hunting encampment. The giants entered the camp at night, rattled pots and pans, and made other mischief, but they were never threatening or showed any malice toward the hunters.

During these playful adventures, the beasts bantered among themselves in a strange, high-pitched language that the hunters named "samurai chatter." All of this occurred just out of sight of the campers, the creatures never showing themselves. The author often recorded the strange chatter and even had it analyzed to determine phonetic structures in an attempt to decipher the meaning of certain phrases. The really cool part of the book is that it includes a CD of actual recordings made on those harrowing and exciting nights.

Many pages have been written about eyewitness sightings and subsequent investigations into everything from visual contact, to strange noises, to odd smells, to tracks found, to the numerous types of structures made by this animal. One of the better books of this type is *Hidden Encounters* by Doug Waller, cofounder of the Southeastern Ohio Society for Bigfoot Investigation (SOSBI). Doug is a friend of mine and another fellow Buckeye. This is not to say that Ohio is better than any other state for Bigfoot investigators. It's just that I am familiar with the work of these authors and know that they are quite professional.

Doug covers the state, investigating Bigfoot encounters in a professional and unbiased manner, relaying witnesses' stories in a casual and informative way. With Ohio being one of the premier Sasquatch hotspots in the country, it isn't difficult for him to find these stories and observations wherever he goes. Having been in the Bigfoot woods myself and having found ample evidence, including tracks, structures, and possible artistic expressions, I know that stories of this creature will continue to surface and that people like Doug and others will go on reporting sightings of and encounters with the Ohio Grassman.

THE GOOD, THE BAD, AND THE UGLY

Television and movies have embraced the phenomenon of Sasquatch and its ability to promote revenue, fill theater seats, and sell popcorn. Jerry Crew has done the entertainment industry a great favor by thrusting Bigfoot into the limelight. There is a sizable list of Bigfoot- and Yeti-themed films ranging from documentaries to the theater of the absurd.

Letters from the Big Man, released in 2011, is among the more notable contributions to the genre. This is the story of Sarah Smith, a government hydrologist, who was sent to study the effects of a fire on a forest in the Pacific Northwest. During her adventures, she inadvertently develops a relationship with the local Sasquatch. This leads to a mutual curiosity that develops into an effort to protect the creatures. The story promotes a warm and sentimental exploration of respect for nature.

In 1972, the cult classic *Legend of Boggy Creek* was released. Filmed in 35mm and lasting ninety minutes, the film gives an account of the beast that has been seen around Fouke, Arkansas, since the 1950s and never captured. Although made on a shoestring, this film has grossed over $20 million and has capitalized on the notoriety of the creature we call Bigfoot.

In 1976, *The Legend of Bigfoot*, a pseudo-documentary directed by Harry Winer, appeared. This deals with Bigfoot as the missing link between apes and humans. Using natural footage and incorporating native legends and lore, including petroglyphs and pictographs, this feature presents arguments in a not-so-professional way. Although entertaining, it is not of the same caliber as some of the later documentaries produced on a grander scale. As an early work, the movie does come across as a sincere attempt to understand and classify the species.

Everyone reading this book has probably either seen or heard of *Harry and the Hendersons*, the 1987 film about a family and its misadventures after hitting a Sasquatch with their station wagon and bringing it home with them. The beast proceeds to destroy everything in sight, yet becomes almost a member of the family. Of course, we have the evil scientist who wants to capture the creature for personal gain, but everything works out in the end. Definitely a family classic.

When we think of Bobcat Goldthwait, we think of his comedy routines. But he is actually a fellow Squatcher. I saw him at an Ohio Bigfoot Conference, where he was a vendor. Bob has produced a movie that was released in 2013 entitled *Willow Creek*. This tale follows a couple looking for the site of the famous Patterson film. As their adventure unfolds, they encounter people who don't want them there, and the poster of a missing girl. As they get closer to the scene of the film, they begin to hear strange sounds in the woods. Then something unexpected happens. For those of you who have not seen this movie, I won't be a spoiler. I can say that what sounds like Bobo Fay doing his famous Bigfoot howl can be heard in the background.

On the other end of the scale, we have those who exploit the name of Bigfoot to entice audiences to see their sometimes demented creations. One such film is a 2004 release entitled *Suburban Sasquatch* that has the title character rampaging through suburbia in a bad Bigfoot costume wreaking havoc, as rangers, a reporter, and a Native American try to rein in the bloodthirsty beast. There goes the neighborhood.

In *Scream of the Sasquatch*, from 2006, bad acting highlights the disparity of Bigfoot chasers running around trying to prove the existence of this beast. One wants to photograph the creature, the other wants to shoot it. Needless to say, the antics and challenges endured are not those of ordinary researchers. The only redeeming quality of this film is that no Sasquatches were harmed in the making of it.

When considering bad Bigfoot movies, one in particular comes to mind. In fact, *Dear God No!*, released in 2011, gives bad a bad name. The story recounts the adventures of a motorcycle gang named the Impalers and their war against a rival gang called Satan's Own. Survivors of the bloodbath hole up in a secluded cabin in the mountains of northern Georgia, where a man-eating Bigfoot killing machine terrorizes them. If you are into gorefests, then this one's for you.

A low-budget snoozer named *Legend of the Sandsquash* tries to capitalize on the Sasquatch name and popularity. Released in 2006, it tells of the ordeals endured when a young girl searches for her missing grandfather. She and a group of friends are terrorized by the sandy beast for whatever reasons. The creature doesn't even resemble a Sasquatch, but is described as covered in sand with a misplaced patch of pubic hair in the frontal region. The producers must haver run out of either glue or sand—or both.

And this is only the tip of the iceberg. There are too many theatrical releases, both good and bad, to mention. One thing is for sure, however. Bigfoot will be permanently entrenched in movie culture as long as people buy tickets to see it.

THE BOOB TUBE

Television is no stranger to Bigfoot-themed productions. Probably the most watched among them is *Finding Bigfoot*. We follow Matt Moneymaker and his crew as they enter active areas, using varied and unusual tactics trying to get a response from the elusive creature. The first season of the show drew 1.2 million viewers. It brought Bigfoot investigation into our living rooms and inspired thousands of weekend warriors to hit the woods, whooping and knocking on trees to beat the band. The crew seem very sincere in their efforts, even though some disagree with their methods. The fact that they have inspired so many of us to venture into the woods to investigate sightings and research stick structures and other evidence attributed to Sasquatch is enough for them to gain my respect.

Most baby boomers can remember a 1976 episode of *The Six Million Dollar Man* in which the star, Lee Majors, encountered Bigfoot while searching for a missing geologist. This was a two-part episode that eventually carried over to *The Bionic Woman*, a spin-off of the original series. It turns out that the big guy was a robot controlled by aliens, which doubtless satisfied viewer appetites for several different fantasy genres.

And we all remember *Fantasy Island*, with Mr. Rourke, played by Ricardo Montalban, and Tattoo, played by Hervé Villechaize. Tattoo began each episode by looking into the sky and yelling, "The plane, the plane!" Mr. Rourke granted wishes to those wanting to act out their fantasies—hence the island's moniker—but always added a life lesson for extra measure. One fantasy articulated by a big game hunter was to hunt Bigfoot. As the episode developed, the hunter learned that the beast had a family, so he decided in the end not to kill it. Thus the life lesson.

In 1976, a children's show named *The Krofft Supershow* aired a fifteen-minute segment called "Bigfoot and Wildboy," about a Bigfoot who raised a human boy and how they fought crime together. This was so popular that it became a series in 1979 and ran for twenty-eight episodes.

And who could possibly forget the *Harry and the Hendersons* TV series from 1991? A spin-off of the popular film, this recounted the continuing adventures of the fish-out-of-water Bigfoot in the modern world.

DOCUMENTARIES

With the growing popularity of all things Bigfoot, an effort was made to determine whether the creature really existed. This brought about a flurry of documentaries that tried to answer this question. In the mid-1970s, a TV show called *In Search of,* narrated by Leonard Nimoy, addressed the strange and unknown, tackling many subjects, including Bigfoot. With true facts lacking, the show relied on eyewitness accounts, along with any evidence produced, like plaster casts of tracks. Mr. Nimoy also hosted a show called *A&E Ancient Mysteries*, which broached the subject of Sasquatch in a similar manner, airing interviews of witnesses throughout the Pacific Northwest where most of the sightings seem to take place. The locations were studied and the incidents dramatized to show the effect these sightings had on those who witnessed them.

The mid-1970s also brought us *Mysterious Monsters*, hosted by Peter Graves, who was famous for his *Mission Impossible* series. This show presented cryptids and monsters in a darker and more sinister light. Eyewitness accounts contain stories of people who were frightened or threatened somehow by these mysterious monsters. A lot of these stories were reenacted for effect.

In 2002, the Travel Channel produced a documentary entitled *Bigfootville*, which told the story of journalist Cindy Bear's attempts to learn the truth about this creature. She interviewed a game warden who stated that anything like this creature would leave sign in the woods, and he hadn't seen anything to prove the creature was real. She and a team of researchers rented a cabin in the woods and set up various forms of surveillance equipment. That night, there was an ice storm that put a damper on their efforts. (You would think they would have checked the weather.) In another segment, she and a couple of witnesses who claimed to have had an encounter with the beast went way back in the woods at night, following a treacherous road in four-wheel-drive vehicles to reach the spot of the sighting. Once there, something threw rocks at them and several in the group saw a dark figure moving back and forth by a tree. One of the witnesses had a pistol and fired a couple of rounds, not intending to hit anything, but to chase the thing away. The group was left with the impression that they had had a real encounter and this creature may exist in southeast Oklahoma.

In 1987, Lifetime Network brought us *Unsolved Mysteries*, originally hosted by Robert Stack. This anthology series presented evidence of assorted mysteries and asked the general public for information to help solve them. A toll-free telephone number was posted for those with information pertaining to certain episodes. Needless to say, the mystery remains.

Bigfoot, Tracking a Legend, a documentary from 2013, follows cryptozoologist Tom Marcum as he investigates Bigfoot sightings in his native Kentucky. Several of the encounters occurred close to where he lives. He embarks on investigations following up on eyewitness accounts of activity in the forest and back hollows in an effort to identify this elusive creature. One of the stories is about Daniel Boone, who killed what he called a Yahoo, which is described as being a Bigfoot-type beast, somewhere in the backwoods of Kentucky.

A 2015 documentary tells a story from my home state of Ohio about the Minerva Monster. It deals with an encounter by the Cayton family in August 1978. Minerva, which is east of Canton, lies within the Bigfoot triangle of Ohio, which includes the hotspot of Salt Fork State Park. The family tells of a terrifying encounter with the beast, which was reported in newspapers all across the country. This case was never solved, as few such cases are, and remains in the realm of the unexplained.

The History Channel aired a series that chronicled unexplained creatures and devoted several episodes to Sasquatch. *MonsterQuest* began in 2007 and was canceled in 2010. The episodes that pertained to Sasquatch were "Bigfoot in New York," which investigated Bigfoot sightings near Whitehall, New York; the "Ohio Grassman" and "Sasquatch Attack," parts one and two; "Bigfoot—Washington State"; "Swamp Beast," which offered insights into the Skunk Ape, said to be the southern cousin of Bigfoot; and "Legend of the Hairy Beast," an episode that deals with Native American myths and legends of the Sasquatch.

The Ohio Grassman episode was interesting to me because it was set in Salt Fork State Park, where I do a lot of my Bigfoot investigating. The segment contained eyewitness accounts as well as observations made by a drone sent up to attempt to catch the beast with thermal-imaging equipment. Although it was a valiant effort, nothing conclusive was found.

MonsterQuest's "Sasquatch Attack" episodes probably presented the best evidence as to the existence of Sasquatch. In these, a group of investigators, including Dr. Jeff Meldrum, went to a remote cabin in northern Ontario that had been vandalized by something other than a bear, a conclusion supported by items that went undisturbed that a bear would have taken. There was a board with nails protruding from it placed on the front porch to keep bears away. The board had been stepped on, as evidenced by the impression of a very large footprint. The blood and flesh samples taken from the nails were tested for DNA. Unfortunately, the samples were too degraded to offer any results.

One evening, a member of the group was peeing off the porch when a large rock was thrown that landed on the roof. Everyone there heard this. Because the cabin was so remote, they ruled out anyone playing tricks on them. They returned to the cabin the next year and didn't encounter anything. There were reports of Bigfoot sightings 100 miles south of their location where the blueberries were ripening, but not where they were, seemingly because the berries in their area weren't quite ready yet. They drew the conclusion that the Sasquatch were migrating north as food became available.

Another installment in the Bigfoot documentary collection brought Dr. Jeff Meldrum along with other noted scientists together for a roundtable discussion. Those in attendance with Dr. Meldrum were Associate Professor Jack Link from McMaster University, Dr. Bill Sellers from the University of Manchester, Professor of Primate Conservation Dr. Anna Nekaris from Oxford Brookes University, and Dr. Ian Redmond, a tropical field biologist and conservationist. The group discussed questions about whether there was enough food to sustain a breeding population in the sighting areas under investigation. Most agreed there was. They also speculated about the nature of this beast, developing some theories that were diverse and intriguing.

One theory proposed that Sasquatch was a relic human like *Homo Heidelbergensis* that had crossed the land bridge from Asia. Another offered the possibility that they were actually Native American shamans who had been living in sacred forests for years, away from human contact, eventually becoming wild men. But the tracks found that were being attributed to

Bigfoot were far too large for these shamans to have left them. The consensus was that this could very well be an unknown ape species living in North America. Dr. Meldrum is of the opinion that this is an unknown species of great ape with limited intelligence. I personally believe that this creature is quite intelligent, perhaps rivaling our own intelligence, as it seems not to need or want to use technology.

Perhaps the most ambitious and anticipated offering is the *Survivorman, Bigfoot* series, which makes a comprehensive and practical attempt to discover this beast. Les Stroud, the Survivorman, had a strange encounter while doing survival trials in Alaska. On five different occasions, he heard what he described as vocalizations by an ape-like animal. He noticed that the trees or brush nearby were moving erratically. As he reached for his camera, there was a sudden crashing in the woods, as if something quite large were making a hasty exit. Les had been on survival outings all over the world, but he had never encountered anything like it. He considered whether this could be a Sasquatch and was determined to find out more.

Les went to Alberta, Canada, where he met up with Bigfoot enthusiast Todd Standing. The pair encountered elaborate stick structures that were attributed to Bigfoot. Along with the structures, they found unusual tracks and heard strange whoops in the distance. On several occasions, they heard what Todd said were tree knocks, which is a supposed form of communication or location tactic used by Bigfoot. While walking a logging road, Les found trees that were embedded in the ground upside down, with the root base skyward. This has been identified as a way Bigfoot marks its territory.

I have actually encountered these in Oregon, which originally sparked my interest in Bigfoot. Les left food gifts like apples. They were gone the next day, and huge tracks were found in the bait area.

In subsequent episodes, Les had more encounters that created genuinely fearful situations. Throughout the experiences, Les always maintained a skeptical and disciplined attitude, not jumping to conclusions and weighing all evidence for credibility. With all of his experiences in what are Bigfoot-active areas, the creature always remained just out of sight, which adds to the enigma.

SOCIAL EVENTS AND SOCIAL MEDIA

Since the discovery of tracks by Jerry Crew, the snowball effect of all things Bigfoot has taken many directions, including organized events orchestrated to share information and sell products. In every state that has had sightings, there are Bigfoot conferences and related festivals. In my home state of Ohio, the Ohio Bigfoot Conference is held at the Salt Fork State Park Lodge each spring. This event draws a large crowd and boasts many speakers who are well-known in the Bigfoot field. I have been a vendor there quite a few times, selling my books and other items. The vendors range from authors offering their works to those selling Bigfoot jewelry and other items, including replica Bigfoot footprint casts. And remember the lady who sells Bigfoot cookies.

Other events include Creature Weekend, which is held near Cambridge, Ohio, Bigfoot Adventure Weekend, Squatch Fest in Loudonville, Ohio, and Minerva Monster Day, which celebrates the Minerva Monster mentioned before. These conferences and festivals are both fun and informative. Check in your state for information concerning similar events. They are well worth your time and effort.

In the age of social media, Facebook is no stranger to the Bigfoot phenomenon. There are quite a few Bigfoot- and cryptid-themed groups with thousands of members. I belong to many of them. A lot of them are state-specific, like the Ohio Bigfoot Hunters and the Kentucky Squatchers. Others provide forums for discussing anything Bigfoot. These groups set rules for behavior: no pornography, no bashing of members, etc. I have learned quite a bit from reading their posts and interacting with members. A few of the groups in this category are Steve's Cryptid Roundtable, Sasquatch: All Theories Welcome, and Bigfoot Structures.

There are also groups that use social media to promote radio programs and podcasts. Two of these groups are Into the Fray Radio, and Bigfoot Radio Net. Some groups use podcasts, for instance *Saswhat: A Show About Bigfoot*, and the *Bigfoot Show*. And of course, there are groups dedicated to Bigfoot television series. *Survivorman-Bigfoot*, *Finding Bigfoot*, and *Mountain Monsters* all have a following on social media. And it's not only Bigfoot that has caught the attention of this media. You can find groups for just about anything. I will admit that I belong to two *Buffy the Vampire Slayer* groups.

Amazon's search engine alone returns 31,420 results for the keyword "Bigfoot." These include books, movies, T-shirts, sweatshirts, stuffed animals, Band-Aids, lunchboxes, playing cards, beer and shot glasses, action figures, wrapping paper, Christmas ornaments, iPhone cases, fan pulls, pajamas, baby bibs, snacks and candies, kids' backpacks, dog clothes, ice cream makers, soap, keychains, coffee mugs, socks, doormats, guitar picks—and the list goes on and on. In fact, Bigfoot has become such a household name and so recognizable that it's easy to market products like novelty or gift items. If there weren't a profit to be made, these items would soon be replaced by those that do sell. Needless to say, Bigfoot branding is a multi-million-dollar industry, and it all goes back to that fateful day and Jerry Crew. I ponder this as I sit here in my Bigfoot pajamas, sipping coffee out of my Bigfoot mug, and munching on a Bigfoot cookie.

THE DARK SIDE

On the darker side of the Bigfoot phenomena, we encounter conspiracy theories that claim the government is hiding information about this creature from the general public for whatever reasons. Some believe they do it to protect the logging industry or to hide the fact that knowledge of these creatures could change established scientific dogma about the origins of humans. Others believe that Bigfoots are aliens or hybrids created by the government, even though they have been reported for hundreds of years. The government moves in mysterious ways. And when it comes to them covering up Bigfoot activity, there does seem to be something going on.

Author William Jevning was called upon to investigate tracks that had been found by hunters in the Mount Adams area of Washington State. They passed US Forest Service rangers as they went to investigate. Upon arrival at the site, they found that the tracks had been deliberately washed away, seemingly by the Forest Service. There are stories on the Internet of the US military recovering bodies and even killing Bigfoots. During a fire in 1999 at Battle Mountain in Nevada, a government employee reported seeing an injured Bigfoot being captured by firefighters and transported out by government vehicles. Everyone involved was instructed to keep quiet. There is a lot of chatter on the Internet concerning cover-ups and conspiracies, but how much is true is anyone's guess.

I do have first-hand knowledge concerning the government covering up Bigfoot activity. I have been investigating several Bigfoot-active areas in Salt Fork State Park in eastern Ohio for several years. In one area where I have found structures and tracks, there was a stand of pines with several, but not all, of the trees bent to make arches. I thought this could be caused by snow load, but we don't normally get that much snow in Ohio, only about thirty-six inches a season. The fact that only a handful of trees were arched was strange. Over time, the arched pine trees became woven together at the top. There was no rope or binding materials used. This was masterfully done. The pines were off the beaten track, so it is unlikely that humans did this. And even if they did, I'm sure they would have used ropes. This leaves the only other creature in the woods with hands, Bigfoot.

I believe this could have been a form of artistic expression, since it didn't seem to have anything to do with shelter or survival. I went back to the site in August 2016, and the woven tree structure had been destroyed. I could see tracks left by heavy equipment. This was state property, so this was either done by the state or contracted by the state, perhaps to cover up Bigfoot activity. There was no other reason to destroy the trees. I had found two nests in the park that also disappeared, but I can't prove it was government activity.

Figure 17. Incredible woven tree structure attributed to Bigfoot. I believe this could be an artistic expression. Unfortunately, this was destroyed by heavy equipment, probably to cover up Bigfoot activity.

The tracks found by Jerry Crew have led us down a path that will continue until this creature is either proven to exist or finally dismissed as folklore. Whatever the outcome, the enigma of Sasquatch will always persist, as it is part of our heritage, as it was in centuries past.

EPILOGUE

Whether our stewardship of this planet was given by the grace of God, by the grace of nature, or just by natural selection, we haven't done very well. We pollute the oceans and the air, pump greenhouse gases into the atmosphere increasing global warming, and encroach on natural habitats. We may be nature's great experiment, but, since we are the only species out of millions that alters nature and creates its own environment using technologies we have developed, the experiment may turn out to be a failure. If we don't organize and prove nature wrong by fixing what we have done, if we don't start to live within nature, we may not survive. And our replacements may be hiding in the wings, waiting to take over and make things right. The hairy giants just may be given the chance to emerge triumphant after we're gone.

REFERENCES

Books

Voices in the Wilderness, Ron Morehead

Sasquatch: Legend Meets Science, Jeff Meldrum

Visits From the Forest People, Julie Scott

The Historical Bigfoot, Chad Arment

The Mountain Gorilla: Ecology and Behavior, George B. Schaller

Tell Me What You See, Major Ed Dames with Joel Harry
  Newman

The Ancient Giants Who Ruled America, Richard J. Dewhurst,
  Bear and Company Books

The Historical Bigfoot, Chad Arment, Coachwhip Publications

Raincoast Sasquatch, J. Robert Alley, Hancock House
  Publications

Online

bigfootencounters.com. See article on Sasquatch Phonetic Alphabet.

bushapes.blogspot.com

occultopedia.com. See articles on Chemosit, Hibago, and Maricoxi.

Cryptomundo.com. See article on Daniel Boone's Yahoo.

Wikipedia.org. See articles on the Wallace Line, Almas, Yeren, Batutut, Orang Mawas, Yeti, Mapinquari, Chuchunya, Beowulf, Enkidu, and Gigantopithecus.

ABOUT THE AUTHOR

MIKE DUPLER is a native Ohioan and avid outdoors-man who has sought adventures across the United States and written books on the paranormal. He enjoys trout fishing in Oregon and Idaho, pheasant hunting in South Dakota, deep-sea fishing and gator hunting in Florida, and pursuing bears in Maine and Nova Scotia.

In recent years, he has turned his natural curiosity and sense of adventure to ghost hunting and searching for evidence of Bigfoot, which he has done with all the fervor and intensity he brings to his outdoor pursuits. He documented the first Bigfoot-attributed stick structure in Nova Scotia, Canada.

Dupler started out hunting ghosts, wanting to know if there really was an afterlife. After many adventures in old prisons and dark, creepy places, he has learned that locations reported to be haunted usually are. His discovery of possible Sasquatch evidence while on a ghost hunt led him to investigate this creature in his native Ohio. After several years and many forays into Bigfoot territory, he has found incredible evidence, which inspired this book. He believes this creature is alive, is flesh and blood, and has fantastic abilities. A mythical creature doesn't leave strange structures, foot prints, and hand prints, he argues. Nor does he believe that a fictional non-entity has ever growled at anyone.

His first book was *Death Explained: A Ghost Hunters Guide to the Afterlife*. Dupler lives on a mountain in Tennessee with his wife.

The journey is not over. The truth is out there.